Lay Leaders of Worship

Lay Leaders of Worship

A Practical and Spiritual Guide

Kathleen Hope Brown

LITURGICAL PRESS
Collegeville, Minnesota

www.litpress.org

1   2   3   4   5   6   7   8   9

Library of Congress Cataloging-in-Publication Data

Brown, Kathleen Hope, 1955–
     Lay leaders of worship : a practical and spiritual guide / Kathleen Hope
Brown.
          p.   cm.
Includes bibliographical references.
     ISBN 0-8146-2954-7 (pbk. : alk. paper)
     1. Catholic Church—Liturgy without a priest.   I. Title.

BX1970.B72   2004
262'.152—dc21

2003011283

Dedicated with love

to my husband

Scott Bradley Brown

and to our sons

Christopher and Stephen

Contents

PART TWO

The Formation of Lay Leaders of Prayer

Preface

On Christmas Eve several years ago, amid all the preparations for family and parish celebrations of the birth of Our Lord and Savior, something else was being born. A few weeks before, on the First Sunday of Advent, our parish had begun a weekly Word and Communion service for the residents of an assisted living facility, those who because of physical impairment or other limitations could not come to church for Sunday Mass with the larger parish community. I had led the new service each week because of my role on the parish staff and my training in the ministry of presiding.

Those few weeks had been an adventure for me as a minister. This assembly's average age was somewhere in the mid-eighties, and few if any had ever attended a worship service led by a layperson. There had been humorous moments, to be sure. At the beginning of the very first service, after what I thought was a clear and careful explanation of what it would be, a dear lady took my hand, patted it, and said, "That's all very nice, honey. Now, where's the priest?" There had also been some heart-wrenching moments, such as when, just after that first service, one of the residents came up to me with a sad expression in her eyes and said, "I'm sorry, honey. It's not you. You did a nice job. But this [a service with a lay presider] is just too hard for someone as old as me." I could only hug her and say quietly, "I understand." For the most part, though, the beginnings of this ministry were a source of great joy and eager anticipation, as I watched the number of people attending grow steadily over the Advent season.

At the Christmas Eve service, I was greeted by our largest assembly yet. I was there nearly half an hour early, but the room was filled with residents already waiting, most dressed in holiday clothes. My heart swelled at the thought that nearly all would have required help to be that dressed up. The looks on their faces were full of holiday spirit and anticipation of what, for most of them, would be their Christmas liturgy. As I stood before them and began the opening greeting of the rite, "Brother and sisters, the Lord invites . . ." the mist in my eyes and the lump in my throat gave way to an altogether new feeling of transparency. It was with all of the love, hope, and Christmas joy in that room that my heart swelled. It was not just the prayers of the rite but the prayers of this community to which I gave voice. The words of welcome that I spoke were not mine but the words of the One who had called us together. I had studied presiding, been fascinated by it, and thoroughly enjoyed the art of doing it, but it was in those moments on that Christmas Eve that the ministry of presiding took hold of my heart. It became for me a ministry of God's overflowing love.

Ministry to the elderly was the beginning of my experience as a leader of prayer, but there have been other experiences as well. While serving as one of the Catholic chaplains at The George Washington University in the late 1990s, I presided at a weekday service for a mixed assembly of students, residents of the neighborhood who considered the Newman Center their parish, and people who worked in the area and came to pray on their lunch hour. The opportunity to lead that service weekly over the course of nearly three years shaped me as a minister in unique and irreplaceable ways. My parish work has also provided occasional opportunities to preside at morning prayer, evening prayer, and RCIA rites.

These experiences of leading prayer have been profoundly moving, challenging, rewarding, and formative. They provide much of the background for this book, along with what I have learned from other lay ministers—pastoral administrators, hospital chaplains, professional ministers on parish staffs, and parish volunteers—who have graciously and generously shared their insights and experiences. I have promised them anonymity, but individually they know my gratitude. The settings in which we preside and the size of the communities we lead vary widely, but there are many common threads in our experiences of the ministry of presiding. As laypeople, we have faced some unique challenges in assuming positions of spiritual leadership in the Church. At times we have met with hostility and rejection. Often we have faced the challenge of winning people over. Our overwhelming experience, however, has been an encounter with people who are affirming and welcoming, who accept the gifts that we offer and respond graciously. The vast majority of people in our communities sense the growing need for lay leadership and are ready to embrace it.

Through my work with the Oblates of Saint Francis de Sales, I have become steeped in the tradition of Salesian spirituality, and throughout the book I draw upon the wisdom of St. Francis de Sales. His early seventeenth-century writings were centuries ahead of their time in their inclusion of the laity in the call to holiness. St. Francis de Sales is recognized as a Doctor of the Church because he was a great spiritual thinker and writer. Above all, however, he was a pastor, and his sense of what that means permeates his writings. His wisdom has much to offer anyone who is in a position of spiritual leadership in the Church.

The book is not meant to be an exhaustive guide to the formation of lay leaders of prayer. That would be impossible for one, short work. It is meant to be suggestive, to point lay leaders of prayer in several directions for guidance, resources and skills to help them grow in spirit and identity. It is also my hope that this book can help to open new dimensions in our vision of spiritual leadership. Whether you are just embarking on the ministry of presiding, or well into the journey and searching for some nourishment and some fresh perspective, my hope is that you can draw from this book some strength for the journey ahead.

Acknowledgments

This book is based in part on my doctoral dissertation, and I gratefully acknowledge the input, support, and encouragement of my dissertation committee, Rev. Charles Gravenstine, D.MIN., Raymond Studzinski, O.S.B., PH.D., Francis Danella, O.S.F.S., D.MIN., and Theresa Koernke, I.H.M., PH.D. I am grateful as well to Daniel P. Grigassy, O.F.M., PH.D., who taught me presiding and encouraged me to publish this work. James Yaekel, O.S.F.S., PH.D., provided help in developing research tools. Barbara A. Inzana, a gifted musician, composer, and teacher, has given me invaluable insights about the use of voice. With the support of my colleague, James J. Greenfield, O.S.F.S., PH.D., I had many opportunities to lead the prayer of the Newman Center community at the George Washington University, and I treasure our friendship and ongoing collaboration. Two of my mentors in ministry, Rev. William B. Schardt and Sister Anita Sherwood, O.S.B., have been and remain important to my vision of spiritual leadership. And finally, this work would not have been possible without the support of my husband, Scott, and our sons, Christopher and Stephen; I am forever grateful for their encouragement, patience, and love.

Who Is the Lay Leader of Worship?

Most adults in our Church today are accustomed to equating spiritual leadership with ordination. For most of the Church's history, ordained ministers have led communities in prayer, in the celebration of the sacraments, in educating people in the faith, while also providing individual spiritual guidance. That model of spiritual leadership has served the Church well for most of its history. At the dawn of the twenty-first century, however, the Church faces new realities. There are fewer and fewer ordained ministers to serve the needs of growing communities. Some communities are without a priest to celebrate the Sunday Eucharist. The situation presents us as a Church with a challenge and an opportunity; it is a graced moment in which to rethink our vision of spiritual leadership.

Change has been happening over the past few decades. Laypeople in increasing numbers are being called upon to meet the spiritual needs of their communities as teachers of the faith, proclaimers of the Word, spiritual directors, and leaders of prayer. Those who are meeting this last need are the focus of this book.

While there might have been a presumption a decade ago that lay leadership of prayer was a temporary phenomenon to address a short-term need, it is now becoming clear that lay ministers will be leading communities in prayer over the long term. Where the shortage of priests is an especially pressing problem, lay pastoral administrators, pastoral associates, directors of religious education and parish volunteers are increasingly relied upon to preside at prayer, including *Sunday Celebrations in the Absence of a Priest*, prayer services for the sick and dying, wakes, graveside services, and even baptisms. Even where the shortage of clergy is not yet a pressing issue, in ever-greater numbers lay people can be found presiding at a whole spectrum of rites and rituals, large and small—from RCIA rites to Liturgies of the Word with Children to Word and Communion Services. It is time to address with careful reflection the question of who these laypeople are who are being called to lead our communities in worship. It is also time to address their need for preparation—practical and spiritual—to undertake this ministry of leadership.

In the early 1990s, two documents—*Sunday Celebrations in the Absence of a Priest* and *A Ritual For Lay Persons*—were addressed to the needs of laypeople[1] who are called upon to lead worship in their communities. The documents outline the rites and rituals at which laypeople may preside, along with the norms and rubrics for lay leaders. Lay presiding is a fairly new development in the modern Church, and these documents broke important new ground in instructing lay ministers who find themselves leading communities in prayer. The documents are primarily juridical in their approach to guiding lay presiders. While they identify these lay ministers in terms of who they *are not* (i.e., ordained ministers), the documents do not address the question of who these lay ministers *are*.

Paragraph 21 of *Sunday Celebrations in the Absence of a Priest* says:

---

[1] In these documents, and also in this book, the term *lay* is used in its technical sense, i.e., nonordained. Some of the laypeople who shared their experiences with me are vowed religious.

> Such persons are to be chosen in view of the consistency
> of their way of life with the Gospel and in the expectation
> of their being acceptable to the community of the faith-
> ful.

Acceptance by the community and the authenticity of minister are clearly assumed and certainly necessary. But what is the relationship of a lay leader of prayer to the community he or she serves, aside from presiding? Is there a pastoral relationship out of which the presiding role flows? Are there particular skills such a person should have? Should he or she have theological training? What sort of spiritual formation is needed?

As we realize that lay presiders are not a stopgap solution to a temporary need but a gift to the Church for the long term, these questions need careful consideration. This book is a reflection on those questions, and might be considered a companion piece to *Sunday Celebration in the Absence of a Priest* and *A Ritual for Lay Persons*, for the use of lay ministers and those who play a role in their formation.

Lay ministry, and lay presiding in particular, are new territory in the modern Church, and new paths—juridical, catechetical, spiritual—need to be forged. Lay ministers, and perhaps especially those who are called to preside at prayer, should be mature in their faith and have a strong sense of their identity as ministers. Dioceses with lay formation programs must carefully consider how to promote the spiritual growth of their lay ministers. Requiring a degree, or even an advanced degree, of lay leaders, while highly desirable, is not in and of itself sufficient for their formation as ministers. Holistic formation for ministry, with its emphasis on personal and spiritual development, is a valued aspect of seminary training and religious life, but opportunities for this sort of ministerial formation are not necessarily a part of degree and certificate programs for laypeople. As a result, many lay ministers, especially those who volunteer and/or combine ministry with another career, may not have a strong sense of identity as ministers or a strong sense of the work that they do as ministry. The spiritual life of a minister is the foundation upon which the work of ministry is built, whether the minister is lay or ordained.

Peter Fink has written of his concern that people who are eager to preach the Word of God and to lead others in prayer might be doing so unaware of the serious demands of these ministries and their profound challenges.

> The ministry of the presider involves more than skills. It involves the human and religious truth of the person presiding, and it involves the human and religious journey which the presider must take, both as a prerequisite for and as a consequence of the ministry which he or she will provide. This human and religious journey is the "stuff" of a spirituality for presiders.[2]

Those who minister without spiritual formation might not bring sufficient depth to the task, and when the ministry begins to transform them, as it inevitably will, they may not have the resources to recognize, understand, or deal with what is happening. Leading a community in prayer is not simply a function, but the presentation of one's whole person. The task calls forth not only skills but the depths of one's being. The spiritual life of the minister inevitably becomes transparent in carrying out the tasks of ministry, especially when the tasks involve preaching (and, by the very nature of the ministry, the leader of prayer preaches in both word and action) and leading worship. It is essential, then, that the spiritual life of the minister be nourished.

> Even as God's love defies any full grasp of our mind, so the depth of the human heart stretches beyond all imagining. . . . [A]n appreciation of our mystery, made in the image of God's own, can stir an eager ministry of

---

[2] Peter E. Fink, s.j., "Spirituality for Liturgical Presiders." *Disciples at the Crossroads: Perspectives on Worship and Church Leadership*, ed. Eleanor Bernstein (Collegeville: The Liturgical Press, 1993) 50–55.

service rooted in a deep-hearted fidelity and stamped
with a contemplative spirit of reverence and wonder.[3]

This book outlines a vision for the spiritual formation of lay
presiders, in an attempt to stir that fidelity and that contemplative spirit.

The spirituality of one who leads a community in worship,
which becomes ever so transparent in the actions of ministry,
should be rooted in prayer, humility, and openness to the work
of the Spirit. It also should be rooted in the leader's relationship with the community, for spiritual leadership can never
exist in isolation but only in relationship to a community.
Attention also must be paid to the skills demanded by the
ministry of presiding. Skills and spirituality are never entirely
separable for a minister, since what a minister does is a reflection of who he or she is. Human actions give flesh and blood to
the activity of the spirit. Every movement, every gesture that a
minister makes speaks of his or her own faith, his or her own
human and spiritual journey. Spirituality without skill makes
for ineffective ministry, and skill without spirituality can hardly
be called ministry at all.

Canon law makes no special mention of the necessity of
formation for laypeople who preside at liturgy and preach, but
commentary on the law notes that the quality and effectiveness
of preaching are crucial, and also that the ministry is demanding and difficult. This form of ministry of the Word requires
education in Scripture and theology.[4] Maturity and experience,
communication and language skills, familiarity with the community, imagination, and careful preparation are also necessary.
Leaders of worship must use all of their talents and resources,

---

[3] George Aschenbrenner, S.J., "A Hidden Self Grown Strong." Robert
Wicks, ed., *Handbook of Spirituality for Ministers* (New York: Paulist Press,
1999) 228.

[4] John Beal, James Coriden and Thomas Green, *New Commentary on the
Code of Canon Law* (New York: Paulist Press, 2000) 928.

in cooperation with the Holy Spirit, in order to move people's hearts.

The formation of lay leaders of prayer should have Scripture at its core. Leaders of prayer are ministers of the Word and, as such, need to be immersed in the Word they preach and proclaim. Their formation should also have a communal dimension. There are benefits to the sharing of insights and experience in a group, and the support of peers is something for which lay ministers often hunger. The formation of ministers should also include reflection on the ministry itself. The experience of ministry needs to be brought into dialogue with our faith tradition if it is to be grounded in that faith. Finally, leaders of worship need to hone the skills called for by the ministry. Presiding at the prayer of a community is more than knowing and doing; it is a presentation of a whole person. But a minister cannot neglect the knowing and doing involved in the ministry, as they are part of his or her human journey.

This book begins with a vision of the ministerial identity and spirituality of a lay leader of prayer, and concludes with some practical suggestions for how to make that vision a reality. It draws in the voices of many people who have been called to preside, in the hope that those voices will lend support and insight to anyone undertaking the ministry of presiding. It brings those voices together, in the hope that together they offer new ways of thinking about spiritual leadership in our Church.

PART ONE

The Identity of the Lay Leader of Prayer

Overview

> Once when Jesus was praying in solitude, and the disciples were with him, he asked them, "Who do the crowds say that I am?" They said in reply, "John the Baptist; others, Elijah; still others, 'One of the ancient prophets has arisen.'" Then he said to them, "But who do you say that I am?" Peter said in reply, "The Messiah of God" (Luke 9:18-20).

Few of us would welcome being caught off guard by the question Jesus poses to his disciples in this passage. Knowing that the answer is far from simple, we would want some time to reflect, to consider the many facets of our response. In reality, however, our journey of faith calls us to confront the question, "Who is God?" every day. Our answer evolves over the course of our lives. Our answer on any given day might well be unlike our answer on any other day. God's self-revelation is not only something we are taught, but something we experience within the context of our lives. We learn who God is as we grow in our relationship with God, as we learn who we are.

Our human journey likewise confronts us with the question, "Who am I?" Again, our answer evolves as we journey through life. Who I am today is not exactly who I was yesterday, last year, or a decade ago. Nor is who I am today likely to be exactly who I will be a year, two years, or a decade from now.

Our spiritual life is the integration of our journey of faith and our human journey. Our spirituality consists of the ever-changing, ever-evolving interplay between our answers to those two questions, "Who is God?" and "Who am I?"

For a layperson called to serve the community of the Church, a question within those question is, "Who am I as a minister?" Ministerial identity is multifaceted and deeply rooted in relationship with God, one's self, and the community that one serves.

To begin to consider the identity of lay ministers who lead the community in prayer, let us consider them as ministers of the Word. The identity of a minister of the Word begins with the authority they have been given by the Church to proclaim, preach, and teach the Word. That authority is rooted in baptism, and made specific and explicit in canon law and liturgical rubrics. It also must be rooted in a sense of authority to minister that comes from within. But authority is only the beginning of identity as a minister of the Word.

The Word of God creates. When God speaks, God creates. When God says, "Let there be light" (Genesis 1:3), light is. God's Word is powerful, creative, and life-giving. Ministers of the Word are the bearers, proclaimers and preachers of that Word. The spirituality of a minister of the Word must be permeated with a sense of awe and reverence at the transformative power of the Word. It is the spirituality of one who has not only heard but been transformed by that Word. A minister who would speak the Word effectively to a community must have allowed that Word to resonate in his or her own soul and speak there. A minister who would give voice and expression to an experience of God must have entered into that experience in his or her own life and allowed themselves to be shaped and transformed by that experience. It is a spirituality of openness, humility, and vulnerability to the creative, life-giving power of the Word. Those who would proclaim and preach the Word must allow that Word to run through their own minds and hearts and draw them into the vision that it holds, the vision of God's kingdom. That requires the minister to be a person of prayer, for prayer is the place where such transformation takes place. Prayer is that place where a minister of the Word grows in authenticity.

Besides being a minister of the Word, a leader of prayer necessarily has a pastoral role in the community. Those who preside at worship gather the community, welcome them, give voice to their prayer, challenge them, and comfort them. It is a role not only of leadership but of service. The leader of prayer is called to be part of the heartbeat, the very life of the community. No one is a pastor in isolation. The call to pastoral leadership is a call to relationship with the people of God—to be one of them, to shepherd them, to guide them, and to serve them.

Who is the lay leader of prayer? He or she is a minister of the Word, one who witnesses to the power of that Word, a member, servant and pastor of the community, and a person so deeply rooted in relationship with God that he or she is willing to allow that relationship to be transparent to the community. The following chapters describe a vision of the ministerial identity of a lay leader of prayer that is multifaceted, involving authority, spirituality, skills, and relationships. This vision will shape the practical suggestions for the spiritual formation and growth of a lay leader of prayer, described in the second part of the book.

CHAPTER ONE

Authority

The identity of any minister begins with a sense of one's authority to minister. Authority is the right to exercise leadership or power. For many people, the word *authority* carries negative connotations of authoritarianism, domination, and coercion. Here, the word is used in a positive sense. The authority that concerns us here is the authority to proclaim the Word, reflect publicly on the Word, and lead a community in prayer. It is a charism, a calling, a gift of spiritual leadership of a community.

The authority for lay leadership of prayer does not come from any one, single source but rather a number of sources:

(1) The starting point for the authority to lead a community in worship is belonging to that community by virtue of baptism.

(2) Juridical authority is also essential. For a nonordained person, the authority to lead a community's prayer must include the permission to preside conveyed in the liturgical rubrics and canon law, as well as the support of that community's ordained leadership.

(3) Personal, moral authority is not the result of juridical decision but is the recognition by the community of the authenticity of the lay minister. He or she has taken the Word of God to heart and lives it.

(4) Professionalism is also a source of authority. The authority to proclaim the Word, reflect on the Word, and lead the community in worship is rooted in that community and the minister's relationship with it. This requires the community's acceptance of the minister's leadership and recognition of his or her training and skill. It also requires the minister's recognition that he or she is in turn accountable to the community.

(5) The authority to minister is also rooted in a sense of call to ministry. When a leader of prayer discerns—in prayer and in interaction with the community—that God is calling them to this ministry, their work draws the strength from that sense of vocation.

No one of these sources, or facets, of the authority for lay presiding is sufficient in and of itself. None, by itself, makes one an authentic and effective leader of prayer. Together, however, they are part of a minister's sense of who he or she is.

1. Belonging to a Worshiping Community: Authority Rooted in Baptism

> Though they differ essentially and not only in degree, the common priesthood of the faithful and the ministerial or hierarchical priesthood are none the less ordered to one another; each in its own proper way shares in the one priesthood of Christ. . . . Incorporated into the Church by baptism, the faithful are appointed by their baptismal character to Christian religious worship; reborn as [children] of God, they must profess before [humankind] the faith they have received from God through the Church.[1]

The fathers of the Church at Vatican II wished to give the concept of priesthood its fullest and richest meaning. Chapter 2

---

[1] Vatican Council II, *Lumen Gentium* 10–11.

of the document *Lumen Gentium,* quoted above, articulates that meaning: our sharing in the priesthood of Christ is rooted in our baptism. In subsequent chapters, *Lumen Gentium* describes the priesthood of Christ specifically as it is reflected in the ministerial priesthood, one which has three aspects: teaching, governing, and sanctifying. But chapter 4 explicitly extends the concept of priesthood to the laity, and to some extent in each of these three aspects.

> Since he wishes to continue his witness and his service through the laity also, the supreme and eternal priest, Christ Jesus, vivifies them with his spirit and ceaselessly impels them to accomplish every good and perfect work. . . . Christ is the great prophet who proclaimed the kingdom of the Father both by the testimony of his life and by the power of his word. Until the full manifestation of his glory, he fulfills his prophetic office, not only by the hierarchy who teach in his name, but also by the laity.[2]

Belonging to this believing, praying community that is the Church begins with our baptism. No one can claim more or less membership than another. Moreover, *Lumen Gentium* makes it clear that ours is not to be a passive membership in that community, but an active membership reflected in Christian witness. Each of us receives the gift of the Spirit, present and alive in our very beings. We are not a community divided into priests and "others," but a priestly community. The authority of a layperson, as a member of this community of the baptized, to step forward and proclaim, preach and teach the Word is rooted here. This is not to say, however, that each and every member of the community will have the charism to be a leader of prayer.

> In the Church not everyone marches along the same path, yet all are called to sanctity and have obtained an equal

[2] *Lumen Gentium* 34–35.

privilege of faith through the justice of God. Although by
Christ's will some are established as teachers, dispensers
of the mysteries and pastors for others, there remains,
nevertheless, a true equality between all with regard to
the dignity and the activity which is common to all the
faithful in the building up of the Body of Christ.[3]

Far from being a radical idea in the middle of the twentieth
century, the idea of the common priesthood of all believers is
reflected in the First Letter of Peter:

[L]ike living stones, let yourselves be built into a spiritual
house to be a holy priesthood to offer spiritual sacrifices
acceptable to God through Jesus Christ . . . you are "a
chosen race, a royal priesthood, a holy nation, a people of
his own, so that you may announce the praises" of him
who called you out of darkness into his wonderful light
(1 Peter 2:5, 9).

St. Augustine, in *City of God*, echoes the idea of the common
priesthood of all believers. He says, "We call all Christians
priests because they are members of the one priest, Christ, just
as we call them all anointed because of the mysterious unction;
hence the apostle Peter addresses them as 'a holy people and
royal priesthood.'"[4]

Augustine also believed in the authority of all members of
this priestly community to pray for and on behalf of one another. He wrote, "the whole church binds and looses the bonds
of sin . . . whoever is bound is separated from your community, and whoever is separated from your community is bound
by you; and when the sinner is reconciled, he is loosed by you,
because you, too, pray to God for him.[5]

A minister's authority to lead a community in prayer begins
with his or her membership in that community. We can give

---

[3] *Lumen Gentium* 32.
[4] St. Augustine, *City of God* 20.10.
[5] St. Augustine, *Sermo post Maurinos* 16.2.

voice to the prayer of the community because we are part of that community. Our membership in the community is not more or less than anyone else's; we simply stand in solidarity with our sisters and brothers in the community of the Church. Our belonging to that community takes a particular, active form of leadership when we use our gifts to give voice to the prayer of God's people.

2. Juridical Authority

> By virtue of baptism and confirmation, lay members of the Christian faithful are witnesses of the gospel message by word and the example of a Christian life; they can also be called upon to cooperate with the bishop and presbyters in the exercise of the ministry of the Word (Code of Canon Law, 759).

By juridical authority, what is meant here is the official permission of the Church to teach, to preach, and to proclaim the Word at liturgy. Juridical authority can take the form of canon law such as the canon noted above, liturgical rubrics, or other ecclesial instruction. It may or may not be marked by a formal ceremony of commissioning.

In order to begin considering juridical authority to lead communities in worship, it is important to go back to a time in the Church when there was no ordained priesthood. In the Acts of the Apostles, early Christian communities were described as praying communities.

> They devoted themselves to the teaching of the apostles and to the communal life, to the breaking of the bread, and to the prayers. . . . Every day they devoted themselves to meeting together in the temple area and to breaking bread in their homes. They ate their meals with exultation and sincerity of heart, praising God and enjoying favor with all the people (Acts 2:42, 46-47).

While these passages make no mention of a ministerial priesthood, it reasonable to assume that someone led the community in prayer. David Power writes that the breaking of bread mentioned in Acts most likely refers to a specific ritual that expressed the nature and unity of the community, not just the meal taken in common. It is likely, Power believes, that the term refers to a blessing and breaking of bread that in the Jewish tradition preceded a meal. The Jewish custom was that the meal did not begin before the father of the family had said a blessing, broken bread, and passed the bread around the table. In the writings of Luke, the ritual was connected with the *koinonia,* or unity, that includes assembly, word (the teaching of the apostles), and the charity that involved sharing goods in common.[6] Since virtually any ritual involves leadership, someone would have been called upon by the community to lead these acts of early Christian worship. Most likely, in the era of house-churches, this leader would have been the host, the head of the household, but not necessarily so. As communities grew, it is not difficult to imagine several leaders being recognized and called upon to lead prayer. However, we have no evidence that this leadership, at least in the very early Church, had any juridical structure.

There was a growing distinction between clergy and laity in the pre-Nicene Church, which accompanied an increasing emphasis on the sacrificial character of the Eucharist. In the *Apostolic Tradition,* there is a description of installation into church ministries in which, for example, readers are installed but the laying on of hands is reserved to bishop, presbyter, and deacon. Nevertheless, throughout the pre-Nicene period, ministry was located within the community, even to the point where the bishop was chosen or accepted by all of the faithful gathered in assembly. By the late Middle Ages, however, the emphasis on the sacrificial character of the Eucharist had dis-

[6] David Power, *The Eucharistic Mystery* (New York: Crossroad, 1995) 27–29.

tinguished not only the bishop but also the presbyters from the rest of the faithful, and leadership at the community's prayer, proclaiming the Word, and preaching all had become equated with ordination. As a result, the Eucharist became no longer the action and prayer of the community but the action and prayer of the priest.[7]

In the Church today, juridical authority is publicly granted in the rite of ordination. In that rite, the community recognizes, accepts, and blesses people for the tasks of preaching, teaching, and sanctifying. For a layperson who presides at the worship of a community, there is no formal ceremony of deputation or commissioning among the official rites of the Church. An individual bishop or pastor might approve a simple rite of commissioning along with prayers for the lay minister, but sometimes there is no such public delegation of authority.

Juridical authority to preside is contained for the most part within the liturgical rubrics. The Sacramentary, the *Rites,* the *Book of Blessings, Sunday Celebration in the Absence of a Priest, A Ritual for Lay Persons,* and other such guidelines give official permission to preside, usually by formulating rubrics with the words, " the priest (or celebrant, understood from previous instructions to be a priest) will . . ." or "the priest or deacon will . . ." Frequently, when allowance is made for the possibility of a lay presider, the instructions will say, "a celebrant who is not a priest or deacon will . . ." An example of this last sort of instruction would be a final blessing to conclude a rite. While an ordained presider may extend his hand in blessing, a lay leader of prayer may not. The words of the blessing are also different for a nonordained presider. Similarly, a nonordained person is permitted to preside at a prayer service for those in a hospital or nursing home, but not to anoint those present.

Specific rubrics for lay leaders of prayer are far more scarce than those for ordained presiders, reflecting how relatively recent lay presiding is in the modern Church. Often, such rubrics

[7] Ibid., 122–24, 166–67.

are stated in the negative, as the title of the most detailed and lengthy instruction for lay leaders of prayer illustrates, *Sunday Celebrations in the Absence of a Priest*. Such negative formulations indicate that juridical authority for lay presiding exists for the most part as a second-best, default option. Perhaps the time has come to see it as a gift to the Church, something to be valued in and of itself.

While rubrics for lay leaders of prayer are being formulated and refined, many still remain vague. For example, the introduction to *Sunday Celebrations in the Absence of a Priest* states:

> The leader who is a layperson uses the special forms indicated in the rites for the greeting and blessing, does not use words that are proper to a priest or deacon, and omits those rites, gestures, and texts that are too readily associated with the Mass and which might give the impression that the lay person is a sacred minister.[8]

Far from being clear and specific, these guidelines are open to wide interpretation. Some might consider, for example, that the *orans* position of the hands during the recitation of the Lord's Prayer is a gesture proper to a priest; others would presume that it simply reflects the role of the presider. The guidelines go on to say that a lay leader is only to use the altar for the rite of Communion.[9] There are no clear guidelines for the lay leader of prayer, however, as to whether or how he or she reverences the altar: a profound bow? A kiss, or is that a gesture reserved to the ordained? A lay leader of prayer can take the approach that he or she should only do what is explicitly stated in the rite as permissible for a layperson, but the result can be a rite empty of the gestures of reverence, welcome, and leader-

---

[8] National Conference of Catholic Bishops, Committee on the Liturgy, *Sunday Celebrations in the Absence of a Priest* (New York: Catholic Book Publishing Company, 1994) 23. It should be noted that this document is being revised as this manuscript goes to press.

[9] Ibid., 24.

ship that the assembly has come to expect. Lay presiders are often in the position of having to make judgments in the absence of guidance.

The vagueness of the guidelines for lay leaders of prayer reflects the fact that lay presiding is still relatively new and not yet clearly defined. So do the apparent contradictions among guidelines. In the *Book of Blessings,* for example, a layperson is instructed, rather than greeting the assembly with the words, "The grace and peace of God our Father and the Lord Jesus Christ be with you all," to use the words, "The grace of our Lord Jesus Christ be with us all, now and forever," to which the assembly responds, "Amen."[10] At first, it might be assumed that the reason for the difference is that a lay presider may not ask a blessing directly on the assembly using the second person. This interpretation would also fit the instruction in *Sunday Celebrations in the Absence of a Priest* that a layperson may not say to the assembly, "The Lord be with you" before proclaiming the gospel, as is customary for an ordained person.[11] However, the rubrics permit a lay presider to greet the assembly with at the beginning of a service with the words, "Grace and peace to you from God our Father and from the Lord Jesus Christ. Blessed be God forever," to which the assembly responds, "Blessed be God forever." One is left to wonder, considering these instructions together, whether the purpose is not simply to avoid having the assembly say to a lay presider, "And also with you." Nowhere is this explained. And nowhere does the lay presider find guidance on what to do when the prescribed dialogue simply doesn't work well. One presider who was leading a Word and Communion service in a retirement home shared this experience:

> I was determined to make the opening dialogue work, with the "Blessed be God forever" response, so I practiced

[10] International Commission on English in the Liturgy, *Book of Blessings* (Collegeville: The Liturgical Press, 1989) 42.
[11] *Sunday Celebrations in the Absence of a Priest*, 133.

it with the people just before the service began. When the time came, though, as soon as I said ". . . be with you all," they said "and also with you," even though I was still talking. When I finished saying "Blessed be God forever," I was looking at a lot of blank stares. I realized then how much people depend on cues during a rite. These people were used to certain cues and had been depending on them for decades. Without them, the rite was unfamiliar and confusing. I think they were wondering if this liturgy was Catholic.

While juridical guidelines for lay leader of prayer can be vague and a little haphazard, they do attempt to make clear the distinction between an ordained and a lay presider. The desire to maintain this distinction was reflected in a 1998 document by the Congregation on the Doctrine of the Faith, "Instruction on Certain Questions Regarding the Collaboration of the Non-Ordained Faithful in the Sacred Ministry of the Priest."

> [I]t is necessary that all who are in any way involved in this collaboration exercise particular care to safeguard the nature and mission of sacred ministry and the vocation and secular character of the lay faithful. It must be remembered that collaboration with does not, in fact, mean substitution for.[12]

Collaboration with does mean recognizing that lay and ordained presiders share a common mission and goal—to give voice to the prayer of the community and to lead the community pastorally and reverently in an experience of worship. Distinctions may need to be safeguarded, but above all there is a need to safeguard the spiritual leadership and welfare of the community.

---

[12] Eight Vatican Offices, "Some Questions Regarding Collaboration of Nonordained Faithful in Priests' Sacred Ministry," *Origins* 27 (24) (November 27, 1997) 399.

This section has illustrated the relative paucity of clear juridical authority and guidelines for the lay leader of prayer, due mainly to the newness of lay presiding at liturgy and the lack of clear definition of the role by the Church. Where there are some rubrics and guidelines, they are frequently "over and against" those for the ordained. In contrast to the authority that comes from belonging to a praying community, discussed in the previous section, juridical authority for a lay presider is scarce, often vaguely defined, and where it exists is frequently stated in negative rather than positive terms. However, no law, rubric, ritual or decree can guarantee true authority, ensure recognition by the community, or move people's hearts. While laws and rubrics are necessary and must be respected, all who would lead a community in prayer, whether lay or ordained, need to look beyond juridical sources of authority if their work is to be truly effective ministry. We need to search beyond the limits of rules and regulations to sources of authority that come from within.

3. Moral Authority

Baptismal and juridical authority are conferred on a minister from external sources. There is an authority that comes from a different source, one that comes from the inside and radiates outward. It is a personal authority, a moral authority that comes from being genuine and trustworthy, from sensitivity to the very presence of God and intuition that recognizes grace wherever it exists. This authority evolves as the community recognizes over time that a minister is who she says she is and practices what she preaches. The inside matches the outside. Authenticity and integration are other words that describe this source of authority.

If lay ministers are not as clearly empowered by juridical structures as ordained ministers, Kathleen Hughes points out that the kind of leadership which they exercise finds its true grounding not in official credentials but in the moral authority of striving for personal holiness.[13] She points out that Jesus had no official, juridical power to speak of, no publicly recognized office. Jesus nevertheless possessed an extraordinary authority that not even his opponents could deny. In fact, wherever he went, Jesus was recognized as one with authority precisely in contrast to those who had official power in the community. There was something genuine and trustworthy about Jesus, something in his manner and message that commanded respect and moved people's hearts. The fruits of his ministry—conversion and healing—were testimony to the power of the Spirit of God at work in him and gave him an authenticity that was, in itself, a source of authority. Jesus did not speak or act on his own behalf, but on behalf of the Father who sent him. His deep and intimate relationship with the Father was the true source of Jesus' authority, coming from inside and radiating outward.

To be an authentic leader of prayer in a community means inviting the One who calls us to minister to be and to move within us. Participation in Jesus' life of obedience and the commitment to bring forth God's kingdom—not our own—are qualities of a minister that become evident to the community. Those qualities become a source of personal, moral authority to proclaim, teach, and preach the Word.

Peter Fink writes that those who speak the Word of God and profess knowledge can be noble or not. The noble ones do not seek to replace God but speak only to help others meet God themselves, to lead others to that place where God alone speaks. Fink suggest this test of how noble the voices are that speak the knowledge of God: God is gracious, respectful of freedom, always inviting and never coercing. Voices that would speak nobly of God can be no less.[14]

Michael Begolly writes that, since all Christian ministry is rooted in Jesus, liturgical presiders must look to Jesus as a

---

[13] Kathleen Hughes, *Lay Presiding: The Art of Leading Prayer* (Collegeville: The Liturgical Press, 1991) 11–17.

[14] Fink, "Spirituality for Liturgical Presiders," 52.

model.[15] Begolly mentions four aspects of Jesus' ministry that need to be part of the inner disposition of a liturgical presider: shepherding, service, prayer, and prophecy. In imitating Jesus, the presider as *shepherd* cares for those in the community with tenderness and compassion. The presider's shepherding role is rooted in his or her day-to-day interaction with the community and response to its needs. Jesus led his community of disciples by example to serve others. In imitation of him, the presider serves the community by gathering its members together for worship, welcoming, comforting, and voicing the community's prayer. *Prayer* was the basis of Jesus' relationship with the Father and at the basis of his ministry. In imitation of Jesus, prayer needs to be an integral part of the life of the presider and lead to a transparent life of faith. In imitation of Jesus as *prophet*, the presider plays an integral role in fostering the community's commitment to justice and peace, and its transformation into an effective witness of the reign of God.

Personal, moral authority as a leader in the community is rooted in the minister's relationship with God, in his or her willingness to be a channel for the work of the Spirit in imitation of Jesus, and in the authenticity and transparency of his or her own spiritual life. To claim the moral authority to lead the community in worship, ministers must live what they pray, practice what they preach. They must be living examples of what they call the community to be. The spiritual life of a leader of prayer is so important that it will be the entire focus of chapter 2 of this book.

4. Authority Rooted in Professionalism

Aside from the baptismal, juridical, and moral authority just discussed, there is an authority that is vested in the minister

---

[15] Michael Begolly, *Leading the Assembly in Prayer: A Practical Guide for Lay and Ordained Presiders* (San Jose, Calif.: Resource Publications, 1997) 64–69.

that cannot be separated from the particular community that he or she serves: the assembly gathered for worship, gathered to do "the work of the people." What is meant by authority in this sense comes from inspiring the confidence of the community.

All ministry in the Church depends upon the community of God's people. Ministry is meaningless in isolation, removed from the context of the faith community. Ministries arise in response to the needs of the people. No one is born a minister, and no one automatically becomes a minister by training, talent, or desire. Ministers are called forth by the community to serve the needs of the community. If this is true of ordained ministers, it is even more true of nonordained presiders who have not been given the official authority conferred at ordination. The lay minister cannot effect anything on his or her own, does not have extraordinary powers, but ministers only as a leader and facilitator of the community's life of faith.

If so much of the authority with which one ministers is rooted in the community, this means that the minister is in turn accountable to the community. This is a relationship of trust that must be recognized, respected, and nurtured. The community must have confidence in the knowledge and skills of the minister. Anything less would violate that trust. Without the credibility that comes with ordination, most lay ministers find that the confidence of the community must be earned. In communities where people are, on average, highly educated, earning trust might require a theological degree. In any case, it requires a professionalism that comes from carefully cultivated skills. One who leads prayer needs to know the Church's rites and rituals with all of their symbols, words, and gestures. The skills demanded of a leader of prayer include facility at public speaking, knowledge of Scripture, and effective planning and collaboration. Presiding makes use of the mind, spirit, body, and voice; presiders pray publicly and with their whole person. Presiding involves skills that must be learned, practiced and honed.

Techniques and skills are essential for the leader of prayer; they give expression to the work of the Spirit. Conversely, nowhere is a lack of personal investment, commitment or enthusiasm more evident than in the leadership of a community's prayer. Skills and techniques are tools with which the task of ministry is accomplished, an embodiment of the spirit of the minister, and a measure of the care and reverence with which the minister approaches his or her work.

It is especially important for a lay leader of prayer to know the rubrics for lay presiding, to be very familiar with and respectful of the guidelines for what a lay presider may and may not do. Initially, communities might be apprehensive about having a lay person lead them in worship, even a bit fearful that they will be scandalized by a lay presider who oversteps boundaries. Being able to answer questions about the rites is important in putting people at ease. It is a reflection of training that people can have confidence in, and a reflection of respect for the Church and its traditions.

Apart from allaying any apprehensions and fears, the assembly is entitled to a rite that flows smoothly. The assembly should not be distracted from prayer by a presider who fidgets, or who pauses to decide what comes next. Knowledge of the rites and rubrics is an expression of respect for the prayer experience of the community. Lay presiders often do not have the formal training in liturgy that ordained presiders have, so they may need to make special efforts to learn the rites and rubrics, and to avail themselves of opportunities to be critiqued. For a lay presider as for an ordained presider, the goal should be to know the task well enough and be able to do it smoothly enough that it becomes not just words, gestures, and symbols, but prayer.

Kathleen Hughes writes that perhaps the most daunting of all aspects of liturgical ministry is its apparent spontaneity, and its effortless flow when it is done well. Flow and the appearance of spontaneity are the result, however, of knowledge, practice, and discipline. Leaders of prayer must learn the Church's patterns of worship and become steeped in the community's repertoire of signs, symbols, words, and gestures.[16] Moreover, they must know not only the details of the rites but what the rites are meant to do; that vision is what will enable them to make reasoned and intelligent judgments when judgments are necessary.

Making effective use of silence can be a challenge for a presider. So aware of what they need to be *doing,* many are apprehensive about pauses and silence. However, an unbroken stream of sound can be monotonous and can actually do violence to a rite. A leader of prayer must respect the assembly's need for time to process what they have heard, to pray in silence, and to listen in silent attentiveness to the voice of God.

Nonverbal communication in liturgy is at least as powerful as verbal communication. *Environment and Art in Catholic Worship* notes:

> The liturgy of the Church has been rich in a tradition of ritual movement and gestures. These actions, subtly, yet really, contribute to an environment which can foster prayer or which can distract from prayer. . . . Gestures which are broad and full in both a visual and a tactile sense support the entire symbolic ritual. When the gestures are done by the presiding minister, they can either engage the entire assembly and bring them into an even greater unity, or, if done poorly, they can isolate.[17]

Presiding involves praying with the voice and the body. An effective presider must be comfortable in his or her body and confident of his or her voice:

> Worship is a human experience, not a set of concepts. It is a thing of beauty and warmth. It is a body-thing, not a head-thing. There is no way for one to think oneself into being a good presider. One has got to get it into one's

---

[16] Hughes, *Lay Presiding,* 19–20.
[17] *Environment and Art in Catholic Worship,* 56.

muscles and bones, just like dancers, actors, and ball-players.[18]

A presider needs to be mindful that every movement of the liturgy is prayer. Walking in procession, bowing, genuflecting, making the sign of the cross, hand position, eye contact, and facial expression all speak loudly to the assembly and need to be done with the utmost care and attention. Sometimes nonverbal communication speaks the loudest of all. Reverent movements and gestures enhance the words of worship. On the other hand, if a leader of prayer moves or gestures in ways that are distracting or disagreeable, the words can be drowned out.

It is important to keep in mind that not everything about leading prayer is studied and practiced. The unexpected can always happen and frequently does. Special adaptations may need to be made because of a recent experience or particular need in the community, or the age or physical abilities of the people gathered. The need for a particular tone, a special prayer, or other accommodation are things that a leader of prayer needs to be able to sense. A presider needs to think on his or her feet, to feel the heartbeat of the community, the rhythm of its worship and its needs at the moment. As one man who presides at a Word and Communion service for an elderly community said: "One of the most challenging parts of being a presider is having to 'wing it' occasionally because of the unique nature of the community." Another shared his experience:

> I was giving my reflection. It was only the second time I presided. I was speaking about forgiveness. One of the men in the assembly suddenly asked, out loud, "What if the Bible says something is wrong and you don't think it's wrong? If you do it, will you still go to Heaven?" I was totally unprepared to be challenged so publicly about

[18] Eugene Walsh, "Training the Muscles that Celebrate," *Liturgy* 17 (6) (1972) 6–9.

what I was saying. Thoughts raced through my mind. Do I now engage in a public dialogue with this man? Do I ignore him and go on? Do I answer him but try to shut it off as quickly as possible? No one ever told me that this might happen!

Another lay presider described this experience:

A woman asked to speak with me privately after the service. I knew that she was very ill and wasn't expected to live much longer. I also knew that she wasn't Catholic, but she came to the service because she liked the community and the prayerfulness. We went into an adjoining room and closed the door. She said that she had been carrying a burden for most of her life and wanted very much to be relieved of it. She told me about a decision she had made more than fifty years ago that she had always regretted and shared many of the details and her emotional struggles with it. I realized that I was, essentially, hearing a confession. Because I had led the prayer service and spoken about God's mercy, she saw me as someone who could assure her of God's love and forgiveness. I prayed silently as she was speaking, "Dear God, please help me not to mess this up!" I used to work as an emergency medical technician, and it was a prayer I used to say often as I went to work on someone when the consequences would be serious if I made a mistake. I really felt like a lot depended on what I said. I was really winging it, but I told her as gently and with as much assurance that I could that I was certain that God forgave her and did not want her to carry that heavy burden any longer. The woman died just a few weeks later.

Dealing with the unexpected is sometimes exactly what a lay minister is called to do. A pastoral associate who is a religious sister shared this story:

I was attending the funeral of my friend, Anne. She had had six children, and I had taught five of them, so we had become very close over the years. Her children were now grown with children of their own, and her husband, Frank, had died two years before. It was a cold, rainy, windy day. On the way to the cemetery after the funeral Mass, I was upset about how the funeral Mass had been conducted. The homily was canned; in fact, the priest never once mentioned Anne's name. When it was time for a family friend to deliver the eulogy after Mass, the priest just introduced him then left the altar!

The car I was riding in was delayed on the way to the cemetery because there had been an accident, no doubt because of the weather. When we got to the burial site, people were huddled under umbrellas and the canopy in the pouring rain. One of Anne's daughters came up to me and said she was concerned because the priest was not there. I assured her that Father was probably also delayed because of the road conditions, but when we stood waiting another fifteen or twenty minutes I began to be concerned myself. Finally, one of Anne's sons came over to me and said, "Sister, could you say a prayer or something, so we can let these people go? We can't keep them standing here in the rain." I walked over under the canopy. I knew that the Church disapproved of laypeople doing this. I prayed, "Lord, you're going to have to tell me what to say."

I began by saying a few words about Anne, her life and her family. I offered love and sympathy to her children and grandchildren. Then I led everyone in the Lord's Prayer. When that was finished, I recited the *In Paradisum;* "Anne, may the angels take you into paradise, may the martyrs come to welcome you on your way . . . and with all the saints in heaven, especially Frank, may you have everlasting rest." Her children surrounded me and hugged me when I finished. Every one of them was crying.

When I got home, I called a priest friend and said, "I want tell someone what I did and why." But I have never regretted it. It needed to be done.

Dealing well with the unexpected takes both pastoral sensitivity and solid theological grounding. A parish pastoral associate had this experience:

> The pastor had vested for weekday morning Mass when an emergency call came from the hospital. Since he had to leave, he asked if I would do a communion service instead, and I agreed. The gospel was the one about the Presentation, when Mary is told by Simeon, "you yourself a sword shall pierce, so that the thoughts of many hearts shall be revealed" (Luke 3:35). Rather than preach in a typical way, I opened the reflection for dialogue. Several people in the assembly shared thoughts about suffering in their own lives. One woman, whom I had never seen before, then stood up and said, "I know why you have suffering in your lives! It is because you have let Satan into your lives!" I saw people cringing at the suggestion that their suffering was brought on by their own weakness and sinfulness. As the presider, I felt that I had to respond. I said, "My dear woman, I don't know where you got that theology, but it was not from the Catholic Church. If there is no redemptive value in suffering, then we might as well take down every crucifix."

Thinking on one's feet in a pastoral situation is an acquired skill. It is a competency born of knowledge of the tradition, the community, and oneself. It is a respectful, sensitive flexibility that takes the best of our knowledge and our tradition and puts them into dialogue with a particular community, at a particular moment in time. It is one of the ways in which leading prayer truly becomes pastoral ministry.

Knowledge of rites and rubrics has been discussed in a general way so far. The more technical skills of public speaking, knowledge of Scripture and effective collaboration will be the subjects of chapter 4. Professionalism that inspires confidence is made up of all of those pieces. Lay presiders have both the opportunity and the responsibility to give God's people not leadership that is second rate, but skillful and effective leadership that reflects dedication and effort.

5. Authority Rooted in a
Sense of Call to the Presiding Ministry

> In the pursuit of virtue, the less we consult our own interests, the more purity of divine love shines through them. God seeks to lead us to a greater purity of heart, renunciation of all self-interest in what relates to God's service.[19]

There is a source of authority for spiritual leadership that comes not in the language of rules or rubrics, nor in the language of information or skills. It comes in the language of the heart. It is a sense of call to the ministry of leading a community in prayer. It is found in the stirrings of the soul, the voice of God in the deepest part of us, a voice that is but a whisper. It is found in the voices of the people around us who mirror back to us our gifts.

Hearing the call to this or any vocation requires careful discernment, attentiveness to God's presence within us and around us. It takes being in touch with the core of who we are, the deepest part of our being, sensing a stirring in our soul, a movement in our heart. When we first sense a call, we may not necessarily be at peace about it. We may feel uncertain, unsettled. The energy surrounding it might be more tension than tranquility. We may feel reluctant. Discerning a call requires openness and questioning.

Reluctance can mean that we are being asked to carefully, honestly and humbly reflect on our gifts and ask ourselves if the leadership of prayer is something that God intends for us to do with them. A minister who is gifted in many other ways may decide that he or she is not called to the ministry of presiding. On the other hand, God often surprises us by calling us out of

---

[19] Francis de Sales, *Introduction to the Devout Life* IV.14–15.

our comfort zone. If our reluctance comes from a hesitancy to be stretched, perhaps we are being asked to trust that God is with us and will give us what we need. Ultimately, discerning a call means being at peace with how we respond, and that peace will come only after overcoming our initial hesitations and facing the truth about ourselves.

One parish minister described her first experience as a presider:

> When the pastor asked me to preside at evening prayer, I told him I was petrified. He said, "What could happen?!" I said, "I could die of fright, that's what could happen!" But I knew that it was my turn and I agreed. When the time came and I was up there in front of the assembly, I looked out and saw the pastor in the back of the church, smiling. I looked around and saw so many people that I knew. A close friend sat in the front row, and she smiled up at me. I felt affirmed at that moment, as though God was saying, "I am with you." I felt called to do this. The whole experience was a gift from God. After that, it just got better and better. Now I'm not afraid anymore. I can embrace it.

Facing truth means being honest with ourselves about our motives. It is God's will that we must discern, not our own. Presiding at prayer can be a heady experience. It puts us in the spotlight and, while some find that intimidating, others find it seductive. A hospital chaplain who frequently leads prayer echoed this sentiment. She said: "The most challenging part of being a presider, for me, is the temptation to self-importance." Another presider shared some of her own inner journey as she began presiding:

> It felt so good, so right, so satisfying. But part of me was still worried. I wondered if it was an ego thing. Was I doing it just because it feels good? I talked with my spiritual director about it. He (a priest) was not yet at the point of saying that it was a call, but he said that what I

was feeling was an affirmation that it was the right thing to be doing. Once I got through that question, a little piece of me was still worried that it would cause trouble, and ultimately it did [referring to objections from the bishop]. But it didn't interfere with my much deeper sense that I was called from this [parish] community, to lead them in prayer in this [formal Liturgy of the Hours, in church] way. Working through the questions has made me stronger. I am more convinced of my call to lead prayer like that.

Discernment also means listening for God's voice in the voices of the people we serve. God calls us to ministry from that community and through that community, which means that we must trust their honest and sincere feedback. If we are genuinely gifted for a ministry, the community will sense it and mirror it back to us. As ministers, we must be willing to listen carefully and humbly to their affirmation and their constructive criticism. Some negative feedback is to be expected from those who are not yet comfortable with lay people in the presiding role. A director of religious education who is accustomed to leading prayer for catechists, students, and parents said:

I rarely get negative feedback now. People are used to having me lead prayer and see it as just part of my job. Every now and then, though, someone will say, "Wouldn't it be nice to have a priest do this?" At first, I tended to take it personally, but now I realize that comments like that aren't about me. They are about a vision of church, the way a particular person thinks things should be because that's what they are used to.

It is important to filter feedback that is about our gifts as ministers from feedback that reflects the need for time and catechesis.

Even when a call to preside is genuine, is not necessarily something that we will feel every day. This ministry will at times be difficult and demanding. Sometimes the feeling of being called will be obscured by transitory things. Sometimes we will honestly wonder why in the world we ever agreed to preside. That doesn't mean the call isn't real; it means that we need to reconnect with our center through prayer. Discernment is not once-and-for-all, but ongoing.

Many of the spiritual traditions in our faith offer frameworks for discernment. The Salesian tradition, for example, speaks of the "two wills of God" to which we must be attentive. The first is the will of God revealed through the many sources of God's inspiration—Scripture, Tradition, even our own thoughts and feelings. The other is "the will of God's good pleasure," and that is God's will as it is revealed through the circumstances of our lives. Salesian discernment is a process of being attentive to the two wills of God, sometimes dealing with tension between the two. It is challenging, ongoing, and requires both a deep life of prayer and a sense of God's all-pervasive presence. It requires no forcefulness, no rush to judgment, but an open and receptive spirit.

Discernment is best undertaken with the help of a spiritual director/friend/companion. In a relationship of honest spiritual sharing, we come to know ourselves more clearly and in so doing come to know God's will for us more clearly. In a trusting relationship we have yet another opportunity to hear God's voice.

CHAPTER TWO

Spirituality

Each day of our human journey, we confront the questions, "Who is God?" and "Who am I?" Our spiritual life is the intersection, the ever-changing, ever-evolving interplay of our answers to those questions. Our spirituality is the disposition of our heart that results, the integration of our everyday human life and our life of faith.

Because ministry is more than doing, because it is involves all of who a minister is, the spirituality of a minister is of the utmost importance. It is the fundamental attitude with which he or she ministers, the foundation on which ministry is built. It is where the call to ministry and the motivation for ministry are found. It is where the Spirit, through the events of the human journey and through the experience of ministry itself, transforms the minister. It is where the minister's relationship with God and self is put into dialogue with the work of bringing about the kingdom of God. And like the minister's sense of authority, his or her spirituality is a fundamental part of ministerial identity.

The spirituality of the minister becomes evident to the community when he or she ministers. The transparency of a minister's spiritual life is one of their gifts to the community. The actions of leading prayer become an intimate sharing of the minister's own relationship with God. The community is inspired, nourished, and led by that sharing.

The leader of prayer must be attentive to his or her own spiritual life not only for personal reasons but for the sake of the community, because the Spirit works not only within but through. The ministry of leading a community in prayer calls for a spirituality that is humble, prayerful, authentic and open to the movement of the Spirit.

1. Humility and Service

> Nothing indeed can humble us so much before the mercy of God as the multitude of his benefits, and nothing can humble us so deeply before his justice as the multitude of our misdeeds. Let us consider what he has done for us and what we have done against him. As we consider in detail our sins let us also reflect in detail on the graces he has given us . . . a lively consideration of the graces received makes us humble, for the recognition of them begets gratitude.[1]

The Word of God contains the message of the blessings and graces he has bestowed on us. The Word also judges us, confronts us with our failure to live up to its call. Humility, as Francis de Sales says, lies in allowing the message of God's blessings and the reality of what God asks of us to seep into our consciousness. Humility, for Francis de Sales, is about truth—the truth of our strengths and the truth of our weaknesses. The Word calls us to humility. The Word also calls us to a love of God which is lived out in love for others. The Word calls us beyond ourselves to loving service of our sisters and brothers.

> Devotion that is true and living presupposes the love of God, rather it is nothing else than a true love of God. . . . Insofar as divine love enriches us it is called

[1] Francis de Sales, *Introduction to the Devout Life* III.5.

grace, which makes us pleasing to God. Insofar as it gives
us the strength to do good, it is called charity. But when it
grows to such a degree of perfection that it makes us not
only do good but moves us to do it carefully, frequently,
and promptly, it is called devotion.[2]

Put into contemporary language, Francis de Sales is saying
that a spirituality filled with the love of God is lived out in a life
of loving service. We allow God's love to be diffusive of itself.
True ministerial service arises not from our own need to be
recognized, affirmed and needed, but from the overflowing love
of God at work in us and through us. It is a love that bursts its
boundaries and pours forth.

The ministry of presiding is, by its nature, not simply a
function but also a service to the community. To be sure, the
leadership of prayer is something that is done, action that is
performed, but in considering presiding as service the focus
here is not so much on action as on disposition, not so much on
what is done as the spirit in which it is done.

> Before the feast of Passover, Jesus knew that his hour had
> come to pass from this world to the Father. He loved his
> own in the world and he loved them to the end. . . .
> [F]ully aware that the Father had put everything into his
> power and that he had come from God and was returning
> to God, he rose from supper and took off his outer gar-
> ments. He took a towel and tied it around his waist. Then
> he poured water into a basin and began to wash his dis-
> ciples' feet and dry them with the towel around his
> waist. . . . [He said] I have given you a model to follow,
> so that as I have done for you, you should also do (John
> 13:1-15).

In presiding at his final meal with his disciples, Jesus provided an example of the loving service to which presiders are
called. It was not so much the particular act of washing feet

[2] Ibid., I.1.

that Jesus held out to his disciples as an example, but an attitude of loving service. That attitude or disposition should be
part of liturgical leadership, whenever and however it takes
place. That attitude of service takes concrete form in a several
ways: placing one's own prayer life at the service of the community, inviting and welcoming members of the community, being
a source of unity for the community, and in the very functions
of proclaiming and preaching.

Ministers who lead the prayer of their communities allow
their own *prayer* life to become transparent and place that
prayer life at the service of the community. By their actions and
their dispositions, they show that prayer is not something separate from the rest of life but is the true expression of a life that
has God at its center. A minister becomes vulnerable in making
his or her spiritual life transparent. When we proclaim, preach,
or teach the Word, we allow the Word to happen through us as
we become open to the work of the Holy Spirit and to the
community that gathers.

The ministry of presiding is also a ministry of *hospitality*. A
presider serves the community by gathering people together, by
speaking gracious words of welcome in the name of Christ.
Everything about the presider—vesture, movements, words,
facial expression, and body language—should communicate
welcome. The presider is not the sole source of the assembly's
hospitality, to be sure, but the presider evokes the hospitality of
the assembly and is quite capable, on the other hand, of making
the community less hospitable. A presider's own attitude is
contagious.

The presider is the focal point of *unity* when the assembly
gathers. In words and gestures, the presider communicates the
reason for the community's very being. The presider is an icon
in two ways: he or she gives voice to the prayer of the community and stands in the image of the God who calls the community together.

The minister who proclaims and preaches the Word is a
servant of the community. The Christian community depends

on those who proclaim and preach the Word to mediate an encounter with God. Children and adults being formed in the faith depend upon those who lead them in prayer to do it in such a way that it touches their minds and hearts. These are humbling responsibilities of service. Those who lead worship inevitably come to the realization that there is a power at work that is not their own.

A woman who leads prayer occasionally in her parish said: "No matter what happens during the service, I always have a very strong sense of God's grace being at work. Presiding can be a very humbling experience."

The image of the servant-leader that Jesus held out to his disciples captures the spirit that a leader of prayer should have. However, the concept of servant-leadership is not without pitfalls. There is a temptation for a minister to think that, as servant, he or she is the only one with something to give. Presiders need to see the community not merely as those who are served, but also as those who support and heal and encourage the presider and are active participants in the community's prayer. Robert Hovda has written that "there is a special ugliness about a function of humble service that has become a symbol of superiority or even a tool of power and domination." Hovda notes that such an attitude is a strong temptation for people in roles of leadership, and it is an attitude that he calls "disastrous" in the Church.[3] A leader of prayer who has allowed the Word of God to permeate his or her being ministers not with a disposition of rank or privilege, but a disposition of humble, loving service. A woman who presides at a Word and Communion service for the elderly said, "I have a fear, or concern, of drawing attention to myself rather than to the liturgy." A parish pastoral director said, "I always try to remember that it's not my church, it's the people's church. Leadership is not about possession."

---

[3] Robert Hovda, *Strong, Loving and Wise: Presiding in Liturgy* (Collegeville: The Liturgical Press, 1976) 5, 16–17.

A retired pastoral associate said: "In our parish, the lay ministers referred to lay presiding by using the term, 'the view from the chair.' This view always felt to me not so much as something set apart, but among the community. It is, of course, an honor, but it is also an awesome responsibility." Authentic servant-leadership is humble, and recognizes that each person in the community has something valuable to give. If the leader of prayer is open to listening to the community and learning from the community, the prayer to which he or she gives voice will be deeper, richer, and fuller.

Lay ministry, and lay presiding in particular, is pioneering work in the modern Church. Any pioneering work is sometimes painful. Humility is a virtue that will serve the lay minister well at those difficult times when his or her ministry is challenged.

> When meekness and humility are good and true they preserve us from the inflammation and swelling that injuries usually cause in our hearts. If we are proud, puffed up and enraged when we are stung and bitten by detractors and enemies, it is a sure sign that in us neither humility nor meekness is genuine and sincere but only apparent and artificial.[4]

The humility that leadership of prayer calls for is about truth—the truth of who and what we are and the truth of who and what we are not. Through words, actions, and symbols the minister speaks that truth. It is not in a spirit of humility, for example, that a lay leader of prayer would presume to wear a stole, a symbol of ordination. On the other hand, it would be false humility for a lay leader of prayer to decline to wear an alb, a symbol of baptism. It is not in a spirit of humility that a lay presider would make gestures of blessing that are reserved to the ordained. Nor is it in a spirit of true humility that a lay

---

[4] Francis de Sales, *Introduction to the Devout Life* III.8.

presider would deny the dignity of his or her role and abdicate the responsibilities that it does entail.

The humility that leadership of prayer calls for is about truth—the truth of the strengths that we bring to our ministry and the truth of our weaknesses. Our faults and our short-comings, faced honestly and sincerely, are capable of making our ministry more gentle, compassionate, respectful, and col-laborative. Along with our strengths and gifts, they allow the Spirit to live and move and work within the community.

2. Authenticity

> We like to make a distinction between our private and public lives and say, "Whatever I do in my private life is nobody else's business." But anyone trying to live a spirit-ual life will soon discover that the most personal is the most universal, the most hidden is the most public, and the most solitary is the most communal. What we live in the most intimate places of our beings is not just for us but for all people. That is why our inner lives are lives for others.[5]

Henri Nouwen's thoughts suggest that authenticity is the intersection—indeed, the integration—of the private and the public, the inside and the outside, the spiritual journey and the human journey. Authenticity means that the presider's spir-ituality permeates the whole of his or her being. Authenticity means that the Word that the leader of prayer proclaims and preaches has invaded his or her own soul and taken root there.

Authenticity means a life of prayer and openness to the ex-perience of God. The deeper a presider's own spiritual life, the more convincing and effective his or her witness and ministry will be. The community will sense the presider's energy and conviction. If the leader of prayer is open to the movement of

[5] Henri Nouwen, *Bread for the Journey: A Daybook of Wisdom and Faith* (San Francisco: Harper, 1997) 2:23.

the Spirit of God in his or her life own life, he or she can enable the Spirit in turn to transform the community.

The ministry of presiding involves both the faith and the humanity of the minister; not a faith that is somehow added onto humanity, but a faith that is integrated into the whole of the minister's human life. The human unveils the religious; the religious is expressed through what is human. Through the person of the minister, Christ's prayer is humanly prayed, the Word of God is given a human voice, the Good News of the Gospel is given human expression. These actions are part of a human journey that is at the same time a journey into the mystery of God.

> If the leaders of prayer are not at home wandering around in their own hearts, if they are not attuned to joy in the presence of friends, if they have not been startled by the wonder of life or surprised by the fragility of all creation, then their public prayer will likewise be impoverished. If they have not grieved at the death of a friend or been humbled by another's love; if they have not known compassion for the weak, or been stirred by a smile of innocence; if they have not been moved or amazed by all of these, then their prayer will likewise be hollow. If they have not discovered their own emptiness without God; if they have not admitted the reality of their own sinfulness; if they have not grieved the alienation which sin effects . . . then their prayer in the assembly will be empty and incapable of giving voice to the inner prayer of those gathered. Leaders of prayer will be icons of the community's prayer before God only to the extent that they are in touch with the human need and longing for God that lie deep in their own and every human heart.[6]

The authenticity of a minister is inclusive of his or her lay state in life. Their human experiences as laypeople are brought to bear on their ministry; those experiences not only form them

[6] Hughes, *Lay Presiding*, 38–39.

but inform their ministry. A lay leader of prayer needs to see his or her lay state in life as a gift that enriches the ministry. One parish minister shared this reflection:

> I think one great advantage we bring is life experiences. In my work with alienated Catholics I had been journeying with one young woman who was working her way back to an active faith life. She was recently married and pleased to discover that she was going to have a baby. When the baby was born prematurely, she called me to the hospital to baptize the infant. As a mother of five I found that this time of baptizing this too tiny infant was both a difficult and blessed time. When the baby died she asked me to prepare and preside over a memorial service for her son. I worked with her and her husband and using a Liturgy of the Word format, we prepared a service that was comforting to the family friends and parish community members. Preparing this service required much prayer and reflection on my part since I too had lost a child. Our pastor was supportive as he prayed with us as a community member. The service was healing for both the young woman and myself. I think the shared experience is what enabled me to lead us all in prayer for our little angels.

Peter Fink defines spirituality as the integration of one's life of faith with the totality of one's human life.[7] "Life of faith" includes prayer, relationship with God, the claim of grace, the struggle against sin, and the faith, hope, and love inspired by God. "The totality of human life" includes human affections, sexuality, the struggles proper to an embodied spirit, relationships, dreams, aspirations, and desires. For Fink, the emphasis is on integration. This excludes any notion of the spiritual life as being in a realm separate from the rest of human life. It excludes any notion of spiritual life as a mythic overlay that overrides human struggles and aspirations. Beneath this is the conviction that the Spirit not only dwells within our deepest

[7] Fink, "Spirituality for Liturgical Presiders," 56.

aspirations and desires but is ultimately their source. The Spirit is at work in and through the lay minister's state in life.

> According to each one's own condition, [the laity] are also bound by a particular duty to imbue and perfect the order of temporal affairs with the spirit of the gospel and thus to give witness to Christ, especially in carrying out these same affairs and in exercising secular functions. (Code of Canon Law, 225.2)

Sharp dichotomies tend to be dangerous and misleading, but canon law does recognize that laypeople, because of the affairs into which their work and lifestyles take them, have different experiences and different opportunities for living their faith than do the ordained and/or consecrated religious.

Having already said that spirituality must include some element of experience, the idea that lay spirituality is a gift in its own right flows quite naturally from the observation that the lived experience of laypeople is different from that of people in consecrated religious life. Elizabeth Dreyer has written that a vibrant spirituality is one that is in tune with the culture in which it finds itself; if not, the spiritual life becomes artificial, something added onto "real life."[8] This means that a vibrant spirituality has, as critical elements, one's lifestyle and daily experience. As laypeople are increasingly recognized as ministers, there is a need to acknowledge and develop the idea of lay spirituality as a gift. We must expand attitudes about the meaning of holiness to encompass the experience of laypeople. This is not to water down our understandings of holiness and spirituality, nor to limit them only to individual experience; the faith tradition that we share is more than individual human experiences. However, our lived experience is formative of our relationship with God. The day-to-day experience of a layperson is

---

[8] Elizabeth Dreyer, *Earth Crammed with Heaven: A Spirituality of Everyday Life* (New York: Paulist Press, 1994) 26–28.

different from that of a consecrated religious, and the recognition of that difference not only makes sense in that light, but it attributes dignity and worth to the spiritual life and vocation of a lay minister.

Authenticity means a holistic understanding of ourselves. That includes our physical bodies—our flesh and blood, our hungers, our energies. We are embodied spirits. As leaders of prayer, we need to claim our incarnational theology, the notion that the human person is the locus of God's activity in the world. Our spirituality happens in our bodies. Leaders of prayer pray publicly with their bodies—their voice, their movements, their gestures. We proclaim in word and deed that the Incarnation is not just something that happened to Jesus, but an ongoing mystery of enormous proportions. Our physical bodies are temples of the Holy Spirit. As embodied spirits, we need nourishment, rest, friendship, laughter, and intimacy. If we seek to nourish our spirituality, we cannot ignore or deny all of those needs.

"Don't sow your desires in someone else's garden; just cultivate your own as best you can; don't long to be other than what you are, but desire to be thoroughly what you are. Direct your thoughts to being very good at that."[9] Authenticity is about knowing who we are. We come to know who we are over the course of our human journey. We come to know who we are as we come to know who God is. Authenticity is about being in touch with where we are on the journey. A pastoral administrator offered this advice: "Know yourself and your own rhythm. Know what you don't have, because you can't give what you don't have." Authenticity means knowing our strengths and our weaknesses, the gifts that we have to offer and the needs that we have. To deny any of our gifts or any of our needs leaves us less able to recognize them in others, and our ministry will be diminished as a result.

---

[9] Francis de Sales, *Letters of Spiritual Direction*, The Classics of Western Spirituality (New York: Paulist Press, 1988) 112.

3. Prayer

> Blessed, indeed, are those who lovingly preserve the aware-
> ness of God's presence in the stillness of their hearts; they
> will be drawing ever closer to God—imperceptible though
> it may seem—their whole soul filled with the infinite
> charm of it. By the awareness of God's presence, in this
> context, I do not mean sense awareness, but one which
> has its place in the apex, the highest point of the soul,
> where the love of God is supreme, where it is chiefly
> practiced.[10]

The leader of prayer must be present to the mystery of God
working in his or her own life, and this presence requires a
prayerful spirit and a practice of prayerful reflection. Prayer is
that place where the connections between the minister's journey of faith and human journey are made. Prayer is that space
in which a minister becomes authentic. Prayer is that place in
which the minister approaches God in humility, and in which
the call to ministry is heard. Prayerfulness is not just a practice
but a way of life for the presider.

In *Fulfilled in Your Hearing: The Homily in the Sunday Assembly*,
the bishops say that one who preaches the Word is called, above
all, to be prayerful.[11] The prayer spoken of is not prayer along
side of or in addition to the ministry, but at the very heart of
the ministry itself. Unless the Word of God is interiorized
through prayerful study of and reflection on the Scriptures, it
cannot sustain the life-giving, love-generating words that one
who presides wants to offer the assembly.

Prayer takes many forms. At the heart of a minister's life
should be time spent in silence and solitude, alone with God.
Like any minister, a presider can make the excuse that his or
her work is a prayer. While hopefully that is true, it is not a

[10] Francis de Sales, *Treatise on the Love of God* VII.1.
[11] National Conference of Catholic Bishops, Committee on Priestly Life
and Ministry, *Fulfilled in Your Hearing: The Homily In The Sunday Assembly*
(Washington, D.C.: National Conference of Catholic Bishops, 1982) 21–25.

substitute for time spent in solitude, drinking in the presence of God and listening attentively for God's voice. One who leads prayer needs to make time and space for private prayer. For some, the setting might be a chapel or a quiet part of their house. For others it might be outdoors, in the beauty of nature. For laypeople with families and professional demands on their time, such time is not built into the day and a special effort is required. However and wherever it happens, it is indispensable. A leader of prayer must know how and when to meet his or her need for personal prayer time. That time in prayer is where a minister faces the reality of who he or she is and who God is, where a minister becomes authentic, where the call to ministry is heard.

Comfort with stillness and silence is not only important for the individual minister as a way to listen for the voice of God. The extent to which a presider is personally comfortable with stillness and silence becomes evident in the liturgy when silence is called for. Part of the ministry of presiding is modeling silent attentiveness, allowing time and interior space for God to speak.

Prayer with the community, whether one is leading that prayer or not, is also a part of the prayerfulness of a minister's life. Communal prayer happens in many ways. Liturgies are one form of communal prayer, but so are informal prayer and faith-sharing groups. Scripture study groups are not only a way for a presider to be immersed in the Word but can also be experiences of communal prayer and opportunities to witness the many ways in which the Word of God speaks in the lives of people.

We are called to be a community, to approach God as a community, and a minister witnesses to that call. If a presider is able to sense the presence of God in the community, wherever and however it is gathered, the ministry of presiding itself becomes not just a function to be carried out but a genuine experience of God, prayer.

There is also a prayerful dwelling in the world, an ability to make the connection between our everyday lives and the Gospel.

This kind of prayerfulness is a contemplative spirit, an ability to sense the presence of God in all of the people and events of life. It is an intuition for seeing the world as drenched in God's grace. God is always near, always calling and speaking with many voices. A prayerful spirit is sensitive to and aware of those voices, always listening, even in the midst of busyness.

An intuitive sense of God's all-pervasive presence is part of the spirituality of a presider when he or she is called upon to preach. The quality of any reflection on the Word depends upon the preacher's ability to sense the life-giving power of the Word at work in everyday life. People hunger for preaching that helps them to connect their faith with what life demands of them day in and day out. A leader of prayer who senses God's presence in the events of everyday life can lead the community to an awareness of that presence and an appreciation for God's abiding love.

This threefold prayerfulness—personal, communal, and in-the-world—is a way of life for a minister, a disposition of the heart for one who would give voice to the community's prayer. All three kinds of prayer are necessary—no one is a substitute for the others. A presider must make time and space for all three and grow in the knowledge of how to feed his or her soul.

One pastoral administrator said:

> The most important thing for me, in doing what I do, is my personal prayer life. And it is important that I use Scripture in my prayer life. Prayer groups are a great help. Someone who leads prayer needs to be accustomed to looking at Scripture and using it in ministry.

[Jesus said to Peter], "Unless I wash you, you will have no inheritance with me" (John 13:8).

Peter and the other disciples were told by Jesus that they had to receive grace before they could be a source of grace. We cannot give what we have not received. If leaders of prayer would mediate an encounter with God for others, they must first experience God in their own life of prayer.

4. Openness to Transformation

> The sun's rays give both light and warmth together. In-
> spiration is a ray of grace bringing light and warmth to
> our hearts: light to show us what is good; warmth to give
> us energy to go after it. All living things in this world are
> numbed by winter's cold; with the return of spring's
> warmth they come to life again—animals move more
> swiftly, birds fly higher with livelier song, plants gaily bud
> and blossom. Without inspiration the life of the soul is
> sluggish, impotent, useless. Once the rays of God's inspi-
> ration strike it, however, we are aware of light and life
> . . . our minds are enlightened, our wills are inflamed
> and quickened with strength to intend and fulfill what-
> ever may lead to our salvation.[12]

A minister who leads the community in prayer is called not
only to proclaim and preach God's Word, but to be open to
that Word in his or her own life. God's Word is living and active and has the power to transform us. If we are open to it, the
Word touches us at the depths of who we are, summons us and
changes us. It feeds our hunger, quenches our thirst. It challenges us and, if we heed its call, it changes us. It softens any
hardness in our hearts. Being present to the mystery of God in
our own life means being open to transformation by God's
grace. Closely related to the qualities of humility and prayerfulness, openness to transformation means a spirituality of surren-
der to the will and action of God. One lay minister shared this
reflection:

> As a national workshop leader I was often the leader of
> prayer at a penance service. It is such a humbling experi-
> ence when small groups share with one another the ways
> they have been called to repentance, forgiveness, and rec-
> onciliation. It is truly amazing how these experiences
> showed me areas in my life that were in need of this. It

[12] Francis de Sales, *Treatise on the Love of God* VIII.10.

has been my experience that presiding often calls me to growth and change. I have always felt that I received more than I gave.

Openness to transformation means having a discerning spirit, one that is always listening for God's voice, attentive to where God is calling. Many spiritual traditions offer models of discernment. It is important for a minister to have some framework within which to approach the discernment of God's will, but the particular framework is less important than the receptive spirit with which it is approached.

Not only is the leader of prayer called to be open to transformation by the Word, he or she is called to be open to transformation by living that Word in the experience of ministry. Ministry is an encounter with the living God in our sisters and brothers. Ministry itself demands that the minister appropriate and live Gospel values. If the minister is vulnerable to the ministry, the ministry will shape the minister's own life.

> And sooner or later the presider will be drawn to where Jesus himself was drawn: to the One who is addressed in prayer, the One whom Jesus names Abba, the one whose constant fidelity to the human journey Jesus himself reveals. And that place of meeting will be as it was for Jesus himself at the core of the presider's own human truth.[13]

A man who presides at services in a retirement community said:

> The aspect of presiding that I appreciate the most is recognizing the impact my preparation for reflections has had on my personal and spiritual life. What an incredible opportunity to study and analyze Scripture and ask how it applies to me and what I can do, from my perspective, to help God's Word to reach the folks at [the retirement home]. It's probably the best, most rewarding thing that has happened to me in my spiritual life.

[13] Fink, "Spirituality for Liturgical Presiders," 62.

A woman who also presides occasionally at those services said:

> I believe presiding has helped me grow spiritually and in
> confidence. I have learned that one doesn't have to be an
> expert in interpreting the readings; one only needs to ex-
> plore their meaning, be authentic, and be willing to take a
> risk and be open. It has been a challenge for me to find
> that comfort or security zone within myself that enables
> me to share a message.

Each day on our journey, we are faced with the questions
"Who is God?" and "Who am I?" Our answers to those questions change and evolve over the course of the journey. Over
time, God reveals who God is and who we are called to be. A
minister experiences that revelation in prayer, in the experiences of life, and perhaps especially in the experience of ministry itself.

God's inspiration and call to transformation can be heard
in the voices of the community we serve, and in the voices of
others in our lives. Openness to transformation requires not
only private reflection, but discernment that involves dialogue
and accountability. The next chapter will consider the importance of relationships in the life of the minister who leads
prayer, the relationships in which we find the mirrors that we
need and a locus of God's presence and activity.

CHAPTER THREE

Relationships

For those who live in the world and desire to embrace true virtue it is necessary to unite together in holy, sacred friendship. By this means they encourage, assist, and lead one another to perform good deeds. . . . The higher the virtues you share and exchange with others, the more perfect your friendship will be. If this participation is in matters of knowledge, the resulting friendship is certainly very praiseworthy. It is still more so if you have virtues in common, namely, prudence, temperance, fortitude, and justice. If your mutual and reciprocal exchanges concern charity, devotion, and Christian perfection, O God, how precious this friendship will be! It will be excellent because it comes from God, excellent because it leads to God, excellent because its bond will endure eternally in God.[1]

Ministry is, by its very nature, relational. It makes no sense in isolation. Just as ministry cannot be separated from the spiritual life of the minister, it cannot be separated from the relationships that it involves. Ministry necessarily calls us out of ourselves and into relationships with others. It is not simply about function, but about who we are as individuals and as a community. The kingdom of God is brought about not just in and through individual people, but in and through the connections among

[1] Francis de Sales, *Introduction to the Devout Life* III.19.

people. The network of relationships that makes up our lives forms and informs our work and our spiritual life. For a minister, relationships determine the quality and effectiveness of ministry. This is especially true for the leader of prayer, as the ministry of presiding is inherently and highly relational. It involves reaching, welcoming, listening, responding, feedback, affirmation, and support. It must be grounded in love and respect.

Relationships with spouses, children, and close friends are all important sources of the affirmation and support that a leader of prayer needs. These are the most intimate sources of love that anchor our lives. They are inevitably reflected in our ministry and all of the other relationships that our work as ministers includes. Our closest relationships help to form our work as ministers and are also formed by it, and our work should not distract us from the time and attention that these relationships require. When we proclaim God's love and call the community together in love, we do it with conviction because we have experienced the incarnation of God's love in the people closest to us. We also proclaim God's love to those closest to us, and some ministers with families find that they are role models for the next generation. One parish minister said:

> I have had the great pleasure to train lay women and men to preside for the Children's Liturgy of the Word. I do find it curious that not too many people get nervous about the Liturgy of the Word for children. Maybe they don't view it as "real worship," or perhaps they just don't think of it as important. Anyway, one woman whom I had trained to preside and preach for the Liturgy of the Word for children really has a great gift for preaching the Good News. One day she came into her bedroom to discover her five-year-old daughter standing on the bed and giving quite an animated oratory into the bedroom mirror. When she asked her daughter, "Lauren, what on earth are you doing?" The little girl replied, "Mommy (with that tone that says, "obviously") I'm preaching—just like you!" I consider it a great gift to know that Lauren, and

perhaps the other girls who participate in the Children's
Liturgy of the Word, will know from an early age that
women can preach, can share the good news, and do it
well. These girls will not have to use their imaginations to
see preaching in their life to come. They have personal
examples that will be part of their understanding of who
is capable of sharing the Word of God.

While not minimizing the importance of our most intimate
relationships, this chapter will pay particular attention to those
relationships that are more directly a part of ministry. A leader
of prayer has important relationships with the people of the community he or she serves, with the ordained ministers who also
lead the community, and also with peers who share in one way
or another in the ministry of spiritual leadership. Hopefully all
of these connections become, over time, holy and sacred friend-
ships that are rooted in God's own love. Along the way, these
relationships are worthy of extraordinary care and attention.
They can fill ministry with a spirit of love. On the other hand,
if those relationships are adversarial, they can be roadblocks to
ministry, poison it, and prevent it from being done with joy.

Because relationships are lived experiences, the actual experiences of those who have undertaken the ministry of presiding
will comprise the bulk of this chapter. Many ministers who
preside at prayer—pastoral administrators, chaplains, religious
educators, and parish volunteers—have generously shared their
reflections on the network of personal connections that forms
the context of their ministry.

Relationship with the Community

Leading a community in prayer, if it is done with all of the
depth, sensitivity, and richness the ministry demands, is necessarily a pastoral relationship with that community. This relationship—as a body and as a network of individuals—needs
careful attention, reflection, and nurturing. The people of the

community are the reason for the ministry and the voice of its call, acceptance and affirmation. It is to the people of the community that the minister is accountable. Occasional stresses and strains in those relationships are as inevitable as they are in any human interactions, but serious and prolonged strain is a barrier to effective ministry.

In her book *They Call Her Pastor*, Ruth Wallace writes about women who administer parishes and who approach their work with "a pastoral heart":

> These women initially had two strikes against them: their gender and the fact that they were replacing a priest in a nontraditional context. But the reason so many of them scored instead of striking out was that they went out of their way to learn the names of parishioners and called them by name, they visited their homes and got to know the family situation, and they did all of this in a warm and caring way. In short, their words and actions embodied a pastoral heart.[2]

When Wallace interviewed these pastoral administrators about what had been important in establishing a relationship with the community, time and time again she was told how important it is for the pastoral leader to learn people's names. Parishioners affirmed over and over how important it is to them to be called by name. Recognition by name affirms people, makes them feel valued, and wins them over. These women have been given the job of *pastoral administrators,* but their caring hearts, the effort they put into nurturing their relationship with the community, are what makes them *pastors*. One woman said:

> Once, I went into a parish and replaced a priest. That was hard. It was harder to win people over than when I came here and started a new parish. Of course, even here people

---

[2] Ruth A. Wallace, *They Call Her Pastor* (Albany, N.Y.: State University of New York Press, 1992) 50.

had hoped for a priest and I felt that. I was careful to learn names, and I even used their names when I gave them Communion. I stopped for awhile, because people in the Church were talking about all the reasons why we shouldn't do that. But then I went back to it. I decided it was just too important. Now, we're up to 350 families, and it's getting hard to keep up with learning everyone's name, but I still try really hard. And people know that I try and they appreciate it.

Another pastoral administrator said: "I make it a point to visit people, even just socially. When people invite me to their homes, I go. It's important to be sensitive to people, to know where they're at." A parish minister who presides at Liturgy of the Hours said: "Whenever I lead prayer, I stand at the back of the church afterwards and greet everyone. It is something that I think is just part of the ministry. And people's comments afterwards have always been very positive. I have always felt called from this community."

A parish minister who leads a Word and Communion service at an assisted living facility, attended mostly by people who are too infirm to travel to the parish church, spoke about how her "pastoral heart" is touched and sometimes broken.

> Once, after I had concluded the service, one of the elderly people there looked at me with sad eyes and said, "Now what do we do?" I wanted to cry! It really brought home to me that, for many of these people, our visit is one of the high points of their week. What is important to them is that we come to see them, we pay attention to them. It is a ministry of presence as much as a liturgy. After she said that, I helped her out onto the porch and just sat there with her awhile, talking to her. I think that was at least as important as the rite.

As a chaplain at university Newman Center, I led a Word and Communion service at midday on a weekday, one day a week. The service was attended by some students and some residents of the area, but mostly by professionals who worked nearby and came to the Newman Center on their lunch hour. A few weeks after these services—a new experience for many of these people, who were accustomed to gathering for Mass—one of the women in the assembly came hesitantly to speak with me. She said that some people were expressing concern about the prayer that I prayed at the end of the penitential rite, "May Almighty God have mercy on us, forgive us our sins, and bring us to everlasting life." Some thought I was giving sacramental absolution, and they felt scandalized. At the next service, before the closing prayer, I took time to address the question. I explained the difference between the prayer that I prayed and sacramental absolution, and I acknowledged that this is new for everyone. I told them that I respected their right to raise questions and invited them to come and talk to me if they had any concerns. You could almost hear the sigh of relief. What seemed like a small thing turned out to be a defining moment in my ministry there. Perhaps it was because people felt assured that I knew the rules, that they could trust my professionalism. But I suspect that it was more because I had shown respect and care for them and their concerns. I had taken time to tend my relationship with them, and it made a difference.

Relationships grow over time, and the way is not always smooth. Sometimes a lay presider's ministry is challenged. Many people's vision of Church does not include lay leadership of prayer. One parish minister who sometimes presides at evening prayer said:

> In the beginning, it was a big issue for me, worrying about how people would react, knowing that they would

be surprised to have a lay woman preside at prayer. But for the most part, the comments that I hear are all very positive. Of course, one person that I know of wrote to the bishop objecting to my presiding and preaching, and she sent a copy to the pastor, but interestingly not to me. Only once did someone raise an objection in person: a young woman came up to me after the service and said, "Who are you, anyway, that you can do this?"

Once after I had led a Communion service, a young woman, who had looked disturbed and upset all through the service, asked if she could speak with me. She became very agitated and was almost crying. She said that what I had been doing was "the work of the devil." She accused me of being "an affront to everything the Church teaches about the role of women." I knew that nothing I could say at that point would change her mind, she just wasn't being rational. All I could do was try to calm her down. It left me really shaken. In my head I knew that the problem was somewhere in her, that I hadn't done anything that was not permitted by the Church, but it actually took awhile to feel confident again. Being confronted with and working through that anxiety had some positive effects. After reflecting deeply and praying about the incident, I regained my confidence and sense of authority. In fact, I am probably stronger and more confident now because of that challenge.

A lay presider must be prepared sometimes to hear, "Isn't it a shame that Father can't do this?" or "We really should have had a priest do this." The lay presider's reaction to remarks such as these call for respect, sensitivity, gentle catechesis, and the perspective of one who is in a prophetic role. Part of what a lay presider does in today's Church is to teach people about what a lay presider can do.

On the other hand, sometimes a very positive part of a lay presider's relationship with the community is the identification that people in the community make with him or her as a lay-person. One presider said: "Sometimes women say, 'It's so good to hear a woman's voice,' or 'It's so good to hear a woman preach.' I think what each one is saying is that she hears her own voice in mine, and it's so good to have a voice!"

A pastoral heart is anxious to give, to be of genuine service to the community. One minister who leads a Liturgy of the Word with Children said:

> Each week, when I would be on the schedule to preside, I would be so nervous. I would worry about what I would say, worry that the kids would think I'm an idiot. I wanted to do this, but I didn't feel like I was really up to the job. I decided to sign up for a Scripture class, and that has helped. I also try to focus each week on one little thing that I can say that might make the kids think, something they can take away with them. I figure that if I can do that, I've at least done something.

Another woman who presides at the same liturgies said: "Sometimes I am concerned that I have not gotten the message to all the children. I want them all to take something with them as they return to the Mass after the children's liturgy. There's another concern that I have, 'Am I the image of Christ for these children?'"

The desire to give something that people can "take away" is a recurring theme in conversations with leaders of prayer. A pastoral administrator who frequently preaches to her community said: "I was a teacher for a million years (OK, a slight exaggeration), and that really helps. I always try to give them something to carry away." One young woman who presides at a Word and Communion service for the elderly worried:

Here I am in my late thirties, looking at this sea of white heads in front of me. I worry whether I have anything to offer them. I mean, they have so much more life experience than I do. But then I realized that that is something I can give them—words of respect and appreciation for their lives, for who they are.

Another woman who leads prayer services for the elderly said: "My favorite part of being a presider is the thought that maybe during the liturgy a seed is planted in someone's heart that he or she takes into eternity." A minister's relationship with the community he or she serves cannot help but be reflected in the quality of his or her presiding. One parish pastoral associate said:

I had to lead an RCIA rite that included the presentation of the Creed recently, when our priest wasn't available. I was nervous. I had never done anything like that before. But early in the rite, the presider addresses the catechumens as "my dear friends," and I realized that I could say those words from the heart, because I had journeyed with them for so many months leading up to that moment. It took away the doubts I had had about whether I "should" be presiding; the rite put words on my relationship with them.

A parish director of religious education who frequently leads prayer services for the students in her program and their parents sees her role as a presider as flowing naturally from her role in the parish. She said: "It is just part of the job. I feel that the children and their parents expect me to do it. And because it flows so naturally from the job, there is a joy and an energy about it for me."

The desire to give, the heart that is moved—a pastoral heart is one that loves and embraces the people entrusted to it. A presider's relationship with the people he or she leads deserves extraordinary care and attention.

Relationships with the Ordained Leadership

The support of bishops, pastors and other clergy is extremely important for lay presiders. Support in the juridical sense of "permission" is necessary. Beyond that, personal support and affirmation from ordained ministers can contribute to a lay minister's sense of confidence and authority, and as a result enhance their ministry. Lack of such support and affirmation can have the opposite effect.

Relationships with the ordained leadership of the local church can be complex, as they involve issues not only of personality, gender differences, and leadership style, but ecclesiology. It can be challenging to face those issues, but it is important for the sake of the community and the ministry to forge relationships that are based on mutual trust and respect. The key to forming genuinely collaborative partnerships is a recognition that we have a common mission, a common goal of helping to bring about the kingdom of God.

One young woman was about to be appointed a pastoral administrator when we spoke a year ago. She excitedly told me about the plans for her installation. She felt supported, affirmed and blessed in her new role. Recently, however, that same diocese was without a bishop, awaiting the appointment of a new episcopal leader, and neither she nor the other pastoral administrators in the diocese were comfortable talking with me. With the support of their previous bishop no longer there, they felt vulnerable in a diocese where some opposed the very idea of laypeople leading communities, and they did not wish to risk saying anything that might stir that opposition. Not only were these lay leaders suffering from the atmosphere of mistrust and disrespect. It is likely that their communities were also suffering from the leadership vacuum, both episcopal and local. Communities depend upon their leaders to work together in trusting and supportive ways; the opposite can only be destructive.

One parish minister in another diocese spoke about her experience after someone had written to the bishop to object to her presiding and preaching:

> I was called to the bishop's office. The intimidation tactics were unbelievable. He was behind a huge desk, and the only thing on it was a folder that he never opened. I guess I was supposed to understand that it contained a pile of letters objecting to what I was doing. He said that my ministry was "confusing the faithful." I kept hearing that phrase over and over in the course of our (mostly one-sided) conversation. If my ministry is confusing people, then why isn't the solution to catechize them? I wasn't doing anything against the rules!

By contrast, lay leaders in other dioceses spoke at length about the support and affirmation they receive from their bishops. One pastoral administrator, who serves as a liaison to the bishop for the pastoral administrators in her diocese, said: "So much depends on [the ordained] leadership. The bishop and I have a really great relationship. I feel like we are friends. I can say what is on my mind, and I speak pretty openly. He gives me room to make decisions and he supports them."

The night before the first time I presided, I was feeling anxious and nervous. I had never done anything like it before. While I was going over the rite and practicing, the phone rang. It was my pastor. He asked how my preparations were going. Then he told me that the following day was the anniversary of his first Mass, and as he had been thinking about that he thought about the ministry I was about to begin. He talked a little about how it had felt for him to preside for the first time. He wished me the best. I can't tell you how touched I was by that call. It was not only supportive of him as the pastor, but he was sharing his feelings about ministry. I will never forget it. I'm sure that what I did the next day was better because of it.

Lay ministers want and need to know that their efforts are valued and appreciated, and the clergy are in a position to help to meet that need. One woman who presides at services for the elderly said:

I think it would be encouraging to experience more of a sense of being commissioned by the faith community of [the parish], perhaps by way of an annual ritual of sending forth. It is important to me to feel valued by the church for what I feel called to do.

The ordained leadership of a community should recognize, and might need to be reminded, that lay ministers do not have the same public rituals and symbols of spiritual leadership that they do. Some lay ministers feel that lack as a hindrance. Lay ministers often long for some sort of validation of their ministry. A pastoral administrator shared this story:

There is a priest assigned to my parish for Sunday Mass, and he is very supportive of me and my ministry here. I preach, even when he says Mass. He's not only supportive of it, he wants it! He feels it is important. Once, a group of people wrote to the bishop to complain that I was preaching rather than him. It was difficult for me, but no one was more supportive than he was!

Pastoral administrators in parishes where clergy only "visit" must also be respectful and supportive of those priests when they come, use those opportunities to affirm the many and varied gifts of all of who minister in the Church, and never demean or undermine them. Ministers who work in parishes with clergy must do so as supportive colleagues. Competition has no place in ministry.

Mutual respect and a recognition that we share a common goal must be the basis of collaborative partnerships between ordained and lay ministers. Together, ordained and lay ministers can find ways to meet one another's needs for support, and to communicate to the community that their leadership is united in a common vision. The following chapter will discuss collaboration as a skill that pastoral leaders can and should learn.

Relationships with Peers

While there is a growing number of laypeople in the Church who lead prayer, the number is still fairly small. It can be difficult for lay presiders to find counterparts. Moreover, many of those people do not live in communities where they can readily find the support of peers, a common prayer life, or even the chance to talk about their ministry. For these reasons, lay leaders of prayer may need to make a special effort to find and take part in peer support groups, or to create them if necessary. But the support, according to many of the lay presiders who spoke with me, is well worth the effort. In fact, one pastoral administrator said: "There are rumors now that our diocese will be split into two dioceses. We (a group of pastoral administrators, who meet monthly) made the decision, though, that even if that happens, we will stay together. That's how important that group is, how important we are to one another." Another pastoral administrator said: "There is a group of ten of us in this diocese, and we get together every month. It's not a business meeting. We get together for a meal, chat, and sharing what's going on in our lives. It's very important to us to have that support." Another minister, who organizes and leads the Liturgy of the Word with Children on her parish, said:

> For the first couple of years, I was so busy getting it off
> the ground that I didn't think about bringing [the pre-
> siders] together for meetings. But once we started to do
> that, I think people found that it made a real difference.
> We share ideas, and we share experiences, and I think
> people find that really valuable.

Lay leaders of prayer often hunger for support and compan-
ionship. Having a support group of peers, either in the same or
similar ministries, can alleviate the loneliness that can deaden
ministry. It can provide an important mirror, sounding board
and opportunity to put things in perspective. It can also be a
source of inspiration in a ministry that requires creativity and
imagination to be done well. Lay ministers do not usually have
such groups built into the fabric of their lives, as those who
live in religious communities often have. In seeking out such a
group, lay presiders might look to any of the following sources:

- other lay leaders of prayer in the parish or diocese

- other ministers of the Word in the parish

- clergy/lay homily preparation groups

- Scripture study/sharing groups

Even if other members of the group cannot be people who
are working in the same ministry, the sharing and supportive
atmosphere of a group of faith-filled people can be of enormous
benefit to the ministry of one who leads prayer. Chapter 6 contains more ideas for forming such a group and tailoring it to the
needs of lay leaders of prayer.

CHAPTER FOUR

Skills

Chapter 1 discussed how important it is for a leader of prayer to know the rites and rubrics. Other, more specific, skills involved in the ministry of presiding will be discussed in this chapter. The skills demanded by the ministry of presiding should be learned, practiced and honed in order for the community to be well served. Effective leadership, done with professionalism, is both a gift to the community and something that the community has a right to expect.

1. Public Speaking/Communication

A presider uses the voice, along with the body, as the primary instrument of prayer. Effective use of the voice is a skill that can be cultivated. Many new presiders can be intimidated by the difficulty of being heard by a large assembly, sometimes with poor acoustics, sometimes without the benefit of a microphone. Some can become discouraged as they watch people looking bored, or even nodding off, as they speak. Some attention to the use the voice and the skills of public speaking can help to overcome some of these difficulties and give confidence to the presider.

An exercise: Stand up straight, and raise your hand above your head. Be attentive to your posture. Maintaining that posture, lower your arms to your sides. Lower your shoulders and try to release the tension in those muscles. Inhale deeply. Put your hand on your stomach and feel it push outward, as it makes room for the expanded diaphragm. Exhale, and feel the stomach move back. Repeat. Feel the alignment of your body at this point—the proper alignment for projecting the voice. Try to relax the muscles in your throat, the muscles around the larynx, which tend to contract and pull upward with tension. Now speak, using the power of the air in the diaphragm rather than the throat muscles to project the voice. Speaking, even speaking loudly, should not leave you hoarse if you use the voice properly.

Professionalism and reverence are expressed in the way a leader of prayer uses his or her tone of voice, volume, pace, and cadence of speech. Those who lead communities in prayer are challenged to develop a high degree of skill in speaking order to win and keep the attention of the community. We live in a culture in which people hear professional speakers through the media every day and so are naturally more demanding in their expectations of any speaker who wants their attention. All the communication skills of public speaking are relevant to the ministry of presiding. A leader of prayer should cultivate those qualities of voice that gives it variety, interest, and warmth as well as authority. The following are some of the skills important to presiding.[1]

Melody is a word normally associated with music, referring to variations in pitch from one level to another. As in music, it is a

[1] In his *Guide for Lectors* (Chicago: Liturgy Training Publications, 1998), Aelred Rosser, O.S.B., discusses many aspects of vocal variety as they apply to those who proclaim the Word. His insights are equally applicable to the ministry of presiding and are reflected here.

graceful flow up and down the scale. Many speakers tend to allow their voice to move up the scale when they are nervous. A speaker must sometimes consciously relax and allow the voice to come back down in pitch. (See the preceding exercise as a way to do this.) As in music, the goal is for melody and words to complement and enhance one another, so that the result captures the attention and sparks the imagination. Voice inflections—subtle changes in melody—are often important cues in the liturgy, and the presider must be mindful of them.

Timing is a skill that also needs to be honed—keeping the words of the liturgy moving at a comfortable and reverent pace while allowing sufficient time for responses and for silences. Timing involves both speed and rhythm—not only how long it takes someone to get from the first word of the rite to the last, but the variations in rhythm involved in getting there. Most people speak more rapidly when they are nervous, and presiders—especially those who are new to the ministry—must be aware of that tendency. Moreover, what seems like a comfortable pace to the speaker's own ears is often too fast for the assembly and unwittingly communicates a lack of reverence. Mindfulness of timing does not mean a dull sameness, though. When the rhythm is a steady beat without variation, the result dulls rather than sparks the imagination.

Volume is an important consideration for any speaker. The leader of prayer must adapt the use of his or her voice to the size of the space and assembly, being careful to project the voice enough to be heard while avoiding any tendency to overpower the assembly. People in the community will be annoyed by insufficient volume. There is always some competition from other noise, internal and external. Many in our communities are elderly, and their hearing may be impaired; their presence and their needs must be respected. On the other hand, excessive volume can also be annoying and distracting. Volume control is a skill that requires some knowledge of the physiology of the voice and its effective use. It also requires an awareness of the space in which the liturgy takes place—size, distance from the assembly, echoes, presence or absence of microphones—and making the appropriate adaptations.

The leader of prayer uses his or her voice in different kinds of speech in the course of a liturgy. Attention to those different ways of speaking is important.

Leaders of prayer use *ritual language* whenever they preside at worship; they must be aware of how it is spoken and how it is heard. Ritual language is language that is more formative than informative, more concerned with "doing" than "telling."[2] Ritual language is what makes the difference between liturgy and teaching, a rite and a speech. In presiding at the rites of the Church, the leader of prayer uses ritual language to gather people and to move the rite along. Often, ritual language is invitation and invitations must be extended with sincerity and warmth. Because they are ritual words—for example, "Let us pray"—the words are familiar to the assembly; the challenge is to make them sound fresh and new each time. If they become flat and boring, life goes out of the liturgy. If they lack warmth, they do not invite. If they become singsong, they are trivialized.

Dialogue is an important part of the ritual language used by presiders. Phrases such as "The Word of the Lord" followed by "Thanks be to God," or "The Gospel of the Lord" followed by "Praise to you, Lord Jesus Christ" are effective when those expected forms are used. Like voice inflections, they are cues for the assembly. While needing to sound fresh each time, liturgical dialogue is meant to be predictable. It is important that leaders of prayer be faithful to the dialogue in its expected form. The community comes to worship expecting certain ritual dialogues. They lose their ritual power when the expected form is departed from because the assembly becomes distracted. When the expected form must be departed from because the presider is a layperson—for example, omitting or replacing "The Lord be with you"—respect for the people assembled and their role in the liturgy would require that the change be explained.

[2] Rosser, p. 37.

Catechesis in these situations is not just a courtesy; the community is entitled to it. In order to answer the questions of the community, it is important for leaders of prayer not only to be familiar with the ritual forms but also with the purposes underlying them.

Scriptural language calls for a particular tone of voice, because it communicates not just words but the very revelation of God. Even what appear to be simple statements in Scripture have a deep meaning and purpose. In order to understand the language of scriptural proclamation and to use it effectively, presiders should be familiar with the various literary forms in Scripture. The language of poetry, for example, is different from the language of narrative. The language of prophecy is different from either of those. Different types of language call for different tones, different qualities in the voice.

A presider, like anyone who speaks in a public setting, is not usually the best judge of how he or she uses the voice. The critique of others is valuable input, and audio- or videotaping can be a helpful tool. The effort involved in making effective use of the voice can be considerable, but the difference in the quality of the liturgy can be enormous. Presiders might also need to seek help in critiquing their nonverbal communication. A mirror on the wall is not always sufficient. Living "mirrors" in the form of friends or trusted advisors can give valuable feedback. Videotaping can also be a powerful learning tool for a leader of prayer.

A presider must also be skilled in communicating through the language of symbols. Symbols speak to our emotions and our senses, to the deepest parts of our psyche. Effective planning for and use of sacred symbols is an essential part of the ministry of presiding. Leaders of prayer, as the ones who bear the symbols, need to be aware of the how they move people's hearts. Study is part of that understanding. Conversation with members of the community about their faith journeys and their experiences of worship can also provide a leader of prayer with valuable insights. In small faith-sharing groups or in private conversation, people can be extraordinarily articulate in describing how rituals and symbols touch their hearts, and leaders of prayer should listen carefully.

2. Collaboration and Planning

> Unity established within a variety of things produces order. Order produces harmony and proportion, and in things that are whole and complete, harmony produces beauty. . . . For music to be beautiful, it is necessary not only that voices be pure, clear, and quite distinct from one another, but also that they be blended in such a fashion that a right consonance and harmony result by means of both union in the midst of variety and variety within that union of voices . . . music is called discordant harmony, or better, harmonious discord.[3]

For St. Francis de Sales, beauty lies in order and harmony. Note the respect for diversity in his thoughts. There is no equation of beauty with uniformity. In fact, it is not possible to produce harmony without diversity. But all must work together in proportion. De Sales' thoughts provide a wonderful image for thinking about liturgy, or any kind of ministry. It is the sum of many parts, sung in harmony.

Liturgy is "the work of the people." Public prayer, in whatever form it takes, is a liturgical celebration and is never meant to be a solo performance on the part of a presider. The Constitution on the Sacred Liturgy states:

> Liturgical services are not private functions, but are celebrations belonging to the Church, which is the "sacrament of unity." . . . Therefore liturgical services involve the whole Body of the Church; they manifest it and have effects upon it; but they also concern the individual members of the Church in different ways, according to their different orders, offices, and actual participa-

---

[3] St. Francis de Sales, *Treatise on the Love of God* I.1.

tion. . . . In liturgical celebrations each one, minister or layperson, who has an office to perform, should do all of, but only, those parts which pertain to that office by the nature of the rite and the principles of the liturgy.[4]

Most fundamentally, this means that the leader of prayer must know his or her community. As one pastoral administrator put it:

> Know your people, know the culture of your people, and be willing to learn from your people. Leadership, as I see it, is about the empowerment of people. I learned that lesson in a big way when, for awhile, I was [pastoral administrator] at two parishes. I couldn't be both places at once. I had to challenge people to take responsibility. And it worked. In fact, one Sunday I was supposed to be away but at the last minute my plans changed. I sat in the back pew where I wouldn't be noticed and just observed. I teased them that they actually did a better job when I wasn't there!

One of my favorite pieces of music is an instrumental work written for piano, violin and flute. The music is a delicate interweaving of the three parts. Throughout the piece, the piano takes the lead, setting the tone and cadence. Sometimes the piano plays the melody and the other instruments provide background and harmony, and at other times the roles change and either the violin or flute plays melody while the others fill out the sound with harmony. The transitions from one to the other are seamless. The musicians must not only master their own parts, but also listen carefully for and respond to the parts of the other instruments to achieve the balance and precision that make this piece of music a work of art.

[4] Vatican Council II, Constitution on the Sacred Liturgy 26, 28.

Beyond knowing the community and being willing to empower the community, any leader of prayer, ordained or lay, must be able actively to collaborate with other liturgical ministers in order to carry out public prayer. Because the presider's role is situated within the context of a praying community, he or she needs the skill of working with others and collaborating with them. This means leading the community's prayer but not dominating or dictating it. It is interaction that goes beyond delegation. It is partnership. The presider leads the prayer of the community while encouraging all of the members of the community to use their gifts and assume their rightful places within the liturgy.

A former pastoral associate shared this experience:

> Our pastor insisted that all of us on the parish staff meet each Thursday to reflect together on the Sunday Scriptures. He wanted the people of the parish to be getting a consistent message, no matter which one of us they were listening to and no matter what setting. After our reflection, we would have dinner together. I think it really accomplished the goal of a unified message. It also created a very strong bond among us as a staff.

Like any human relationships, however, relationships among the leaders of a community of faith are not without difficulties. As one pastoral administrator put it: "If personalities don't go together, it's difficult. Power plays and egos can get in the way. So can insecurities. The human element can be a challenge." Egos and power plays get in the way of effective spiritual leadership. So do prejudices, stereotypes, and an inability to really listen.

An exercise: Bring together a small group of people, perhaps in a retreat setting, who by the nature of their work need to collaborate. Make the question for discussion a question about which people will have strong, or at least non-neutral, feelings. Pose the question, and allow each person a few minutes to speak their mind. No one is permitted to respond; the other participants can only listen. It can be surprisingly difficult for people not to jump in with "But . . ." or "And . . .," but attentive and nonjudgmental listening is an essential skill for collaboration. To take the exercise a step further, allow the other participants to respond, but only in the form of repeating back to the speakers what they heard them say. This reflective listening gives people a way to gauge how carefully they listen, and also a way to see how different listeners can hear the same words in different ways. That sensitivity is another important skill for genuine collaboration.

This collaborative relationship between the presider and the community begins not just with the interpersonal skills that have just been mentioned but with a vision of Church that is horizontal, inclusive, respectful, and empowering. Collaboration takes form and flesh when liturgy is planned. The presider has an indispensable role in planning the liturgy, but along with the other liturgical ministers. Liturgy demands a vision and all of the choices and creative activity that go into making that vision a reality in a concrete setting. This requires planning. The presider must participate in this planning as a resource for the other ministers, and also to gain the confidence and assurance that comes with knowing what is expected to happen at each moment in the liturgy. This demands a willingness to collaborate and skill at doing so. It also requires active, respectful listening to other ministers who have a role in the liturgy. The work of many people—the presider, musicians, readers, ushers, ministers of the Eucharist, and sometimes catechists and those involved in sacramental preparation—all comes together when the community prays together. It is in that gathering that we celebrate who we are as God's people. Recognizing and respecting the gifts of all who gather is an essential part of spiritual and liturgical leadership.

A hospital chaplain who frequently presides at prayer is quick to agree that it is not a one-person job. She said: "Presiding is just part of a ministry team endeavor. The results depend on participation by all members of the team—musicians, lectors, helpers. All of them are important to hospitality and unity."

Besides how the ritual will unfold, the lay presider is frequently challenged by where it will unfold. In planning public prayer, the presider also needs to have some sense of the space, the environment in which the liturgy will take place. Frequently, laypeople are called upon to preside in a space that is not typically used for worship. The children's Liturgy of the Word, for example, might take place in a classroom or conference room. A Word and Communion service might be held in a hospital waiting room or the common space of a nursing home. Having some sense of how to give these places some feel of sacred space is a skill that is often asked of a presider, and a lay presider in particular. The gifts of people who have knowledge of art and environment, hospitality, and the community itself can and should be brought to bear in making the space for prayer, however unconventional, look and feel like sacred space.

3. Engaging Scripture

A leader of prayer is, first and foremost, a minister of the Word. Public prayer involves the proclamation of Scripture and sometimes reflection on Scripture. The presider should allow the words of Scripture to resonate in his or her own heart. Certainly some formal Scripture study is helpful for anyone who is called upon to lead prayer. But familiarity with Scripture for the purpose of leading prayer is not the same as being able to give a scholarly lecture. The presider is called to make the connection between Scripture and the lives of the people assembled. It does not require a theological degree. It does require an ability to engage God's Word in Scripture. That facility can be enhanced by an individual's private reading and studying, but since it involves public sharing it is best achieved in a group. A small group of peers and/or parishioners who come together on a regular basis to share thoughts on Scripture can be an invaluable resource for one who leads prayer. The coming together and sharing is more important than the specific method or approach that is used, but any group must decide where and how to begin, so a few different methods are discussed here.

One approach to reflection on the Scriptures which treats with reverence and respect the human journey and the importance of spiritual experience is *lectio divina*. Norvene Vest outlines this process in a book entitled *Gathered in the Word: Praying the Scriptures in Small Groups*.[5] *Lectio divina*, as distinct from Scripture study, is a devotional approach to Scripture that is intended not for instruction or analysis but for spiritual nourishment. It lends itself extremely well to self-directed learning and spiritual formation that integrates faith and experience. *Lectio* is an ancient practice, preserved primarily by monastic communities, that transcends time- and culture-specific references, reaching into the reader's own experience in order to facilitate spiritual growth. Vest says that, above all, *lectio* is undertaken in the conviction that God's Word is meant to be a "good" Word, that is, something carrying God's own life in a way that benefits the one who receives it faithfully.[6] *Lectio* is an encounter with the living God. It is praying with the Scriptures. It involves reason and discursive thought, an inner exploration of meaning.

The formal process of *lectio divina* is as follows: A member of the group reads aloud a passage from Scripture. As the passage is read, the group listens attentively and each member of the group takes note of any word or phrase that seems to stand

[5] Norvene Vest, *Gathered in the Word: Praying the Scriptures in Small Groups* (Nashville: Upper Room Books, 1996).
[6] Ibid., 11.

out for them, that seems to be "given" to them. After a moment of silent reflection, the members simply speak aloud these words or phrases. Another member of the group then reads the passage again, and in silence the group members reflect on how the passage seems to be touching their lives. Then, members of the group briefly speak aloud their sense of being touched. The same passage is read yet a third time, and in silence the group members reflect on a possible invitation contained in the passage to do something. Each member may then speak his or her invitation, and the person on their left offers a prayer that he or she might be empowered to respond to the invitation.

The process of *lectio* involves sharing with a group a part of our spiritual life, the deep intimacy of how God is calling and inviting us. The contributions of each member of the group must be regarded as a gift to the group, not a demand from it. As members of the group experience the beauty of the inner lives of the others, a deep and natural reverence for one another grows. Mutual sharing of the experience of God—when offered freely and not demanded—enables us to become more fully who we are. Our deepened reverence for the spiritual lives of others gives us a whole new perspective on our own. The process of sharing in *lectio* also brings the participants to a heightened awareness that God's Word is alive, vibrant, multifaceted, and challenging.

Lectio divina is not a substitute for Scripture study. It does not impart the sort of information about Scripture—historical background, recent scholarly interpretations, nuances in translation—that people who hunger for spiritual formation as ministers of the Word might want and expect. Certainly courses in Scripture would be very beneficial to ministers who have access to them. Alternatives to classroom Scripture study are available, however.

One approach to the study of Scripture which is becoming increasingly popular is *Little Rock Scripture Study*.[7] Participants

---

[7] *Little Rock Scripture Study*, Liturgical Press, Collegeville, Minnesota.

spend about twenty minutes a day in personal Scripture reflection, guided by published materials. Weekly, participants gather in small groups to pray and share their reflections. Lectures are also part of the program, delivered either by local speakers or tape. Personal and shared prayer are the most essential elements of the program. Scholarship and group discussion are also integral. Through this combination of approaches, participants are able to come to a deeper, richer, fuller understanding of Scripture. Ministers of the Word can only benefit from the insights it offers.

Whatever approach or combination of approaches is chosen, those who lead prayer and proclaim the Word need constantly to grow in their understanding and appreciation of Scripture. One who proclaims the Word must have allowed that Word to invade his or her soul and taken root there.

4. Theological Reflection

The experiences of ministry can be profoundly moving and occasionally unsettling. Some incidents and encounters can leave a minister wondering: How do I handle this? What is God calling me to in this encounter? How can I learn and grow from this experience? Theological reflection is a way of discerning the answers to those questions.

Theological reflection is the art and the practice connecting life and faith, putting our human experience into dialogue with our faith tradition. For a minister, it specifically means putting the activity of ministry into dialogue with the resources of our faith tradition. For a minister of the Word, it means consciously reflecting on that ministry and bringing to bear on that reflection the very Word that is proclaimed. The term theological reflection is both a concept and a practice, and the term can refer to a specific method of integrating faith and experience. Some of those methods are discussed briefly below. However, the goal of any method is to make connecting life and faith, ministry and our faith tradition, a habit and, over time, an instinct. Those who lead communities in prayer deepen and strengthen their ministry when they develop a habit of theological reflection on their experience of ministry.

While theological reflection can be done by one person alone, it is best done in a group where people can share their experiences of ministry and benefit from one another's insights. Ideally, it takes place in a group that meets regularly, in which the participants are comfortable with one another and sharing flows freely.

One method of theological reflection is articulated by Robert Kinast in his book *Making Faith Sense*.[8] Because the Kinast method is simple, clear, and user-friendly, it can be learned easily by ministers who have no previous experience with theological reflection. The process involves four steps that are easy to remember with the acronym NAME: narration, analysis, meaning, and enactment.

Narration means telling the story, relating the facts of some experiences that a minister has had. There are two goals of narration: to tell the story as accurately and completely as possible, and to let the experience reveal its own meaning on its own terms. Narration involves asking who was involved, what happened, where, when and how it happened.

Analysis of an experience means asking why it occurred as it did. It is actually an extension of the narration, but now examining the facts in order to gain a clearer understanding of them. Analysis involves asking why these people were involved, why events happened the way they did, and why the situation was structured the way it was.

Meaning is the heart of theological reflection. Kinast calls it making faith-sense. Making faith-sense, in essence, is searching for the spiritual meaning of an experience. This means bringing the lessons and values of our faith tradition to bear on

---

[8] Robert Kinast, *Making Faith Sense* (Collegeville: The Liturgical Press, 1999) 33–74.

that experience. The process involves asking the following questions: Does the experience remind me a Scripture passage, or some other part of the faith tradition? Does it affirm or contradict my understanding of what I know and believe? How does it affect me as a believer and as a minister?

Enactment means turning reflection into action. In the words of the Letter of James, it means "Be doers of the Word and not hearers only" (James 1:22). It means keeping faith alive. It involves asking the following questions: What does the reflection which I have undertaken imply for the way that I live? How is it going to change me as a believer and as a minister? How will I proceed in living out my faith, in light of my reflection?

James and Evelyn Whitehead also outline a method of theological reflection in their book *Method in Ministry: Theological Reflection and Christian Ministry*.[9] Like the Kinast method, the Whitehead method is enacted in a group setting. The process has three steps.

Attending consists of seeking and exploring the information on a particular pastoral issue or concern that is available in a minister's personal experience, our Christian tradition, and cultural resources. Each member of the group will have some of that wisdom to share. The most important skill involved is the ability to listen attentively. In itself, this is an exercise in collaboration.

Assertion is bringing the perspectives gathered from these three sources—experience, tradition and culture—into dialogue. The important skills here are having the courage to share our convictions with others in the group and the willingness to be challenged by them. Laypeople in ministry need both of these skills. It is important that they not feel that their experience, although perhaps limited, is lacking in meaning or depth.

Pastoral response is taking the results of insight and discussion and putting them into action. This is an ongoing aspect of

[9] James and Evelyn Whitehead, *Method in Ministry: Theological Reflection and Christian Ministry* (Kansas City, Mo.: Sheed and Ward, 1995).

ministry, since it involves discernment, decision-making, planning, and evaluation.

Theological reflection situates our experience within a framework of belief. As it becomes a habit, a minister becomes more confident in drawing on that framework, that faith tradition. It helps a minister to "be prepared to give an explanation for the hope" within (1 Peter 3:15). Theological reflection, in whatever process it occurs, helps to ground the decisions and actions of a minister in the context of belief, and as a result those decisions and actions have deeper, richer meaning.

The process of theological reflection promotes a minister's personal, spiritual growth. The Spirit works within each person, within their individuality and uniqueness. Theological reflection is an ongoing task of making sense of our unique experiences in light of our faith tradition, being attentive to the activity of the Spirit in those experiences, and listening to the wisdom that others have to offer. This creative work is a way of growing toward spiritual maturity, the ultimate goal of any program of spiritual formation.

Theological reflection is a skill that also has enormous value in preaching. The habit of connecting experience and our faith tradition makes it easier for a minister to connect a passage of Scripture with the lives of the people in the assembly.

5. Preaching

Frequently, laypeople who lead their communities in prayer are expected to provide some reflection on Scripture for the assembly since most of our communal prayer includes some reading of Scripture. These reflections can take the form of a dialogue with children in their Liturgy of the Word, a few words of reflection on a passage of Scripture, words of comfort at a memorial or graveside service, or something that, if given by an ordained minister, would be called a full-length homily. Whatever form preaching takes, it is the art of making a connection between our faith tradition and the lives of those who are gathered. Engaging Scripture and theological reflection, discussed in the preceding sections, are two of the building blocks of effective preaching. Preaching also calls upon all of the qualities of a presider's spirituality—transparency, humility, authenticity—as well as the ability to speak publicly, the ability to connect life and faith, and an ability to engage Scripture. Preaching is a ministry that is worthy of much time, effort, care, and attention. Reflection on the Word of God is an important way in which people are "fed" when they gather for prayer.

Most Catholic adults today have grown up in a Church where preaching was reserved to the ordained. Lay preaching, until very recently, has been extremely rare and even now it is not commonplace. As a result, lay ministers who are called upon to preach find themselves in a role that is intimidating not only for the demands it makes on the minister but for its unfamiliarity and lack of role models. Lay preaching is not without precedent, however.

> But I want you to know that Christ is the head of every man, and a husband the head of his wife, and God the head of Christ. Any man who prays or prophesies with his head covered brings shame upon his head. But any woman who prays or prophesies with her head unveiled brings shame upon her head, for it is one and the same thing as if she had had her head shaved. For if a woman does not have her head veiled, she may as well have her hair cut off. But if it is shameful for a woman to have her hair cut off or her head shaved, then she should wear a veil (1 Cor 11:3-6).

The point here is not the hierarchy that is outlined, but the evidence that various members of the community, men and women, were preaching in the early Church. Acts 18:26 mentions a husband and wife, Priscilla and Aquila, as having instructed Apollos in the Christian faith. The Gospel of John places great importance on the witness of the Samaritan woman (John 4:4-42) and Mary Magdalene (John 20:11-18).

The authority to preach, a particular form of ministry of the Word, comes from the same sources as the authority for spiritual leadership of a community, discussed in chapter 1. Most fundamentally, that authority is rooted in baptism, but also has juridical and personal aspects. Preaching requires the skills of public speaking, knowledge of Scripture and theology, and the ability to connect faith and life. The combination of skills and insights required to preach well is, indeed, a gift. It is not a gift that comes with ordination, but the work of the Holy Spirit. In cooperation with the Spirit, even the most gifted preachers devote much time and effort to this demanding ministry. The skills can and should be practiced and honed.

In her book *Naming Grace: Preaching and the Sacramental Imagination,* Mary Catherine Hilkert describes the art of preaching as "at once the proclamation of God's word and the naming of grace in human experience."[10] The "good news" of God's abiding presence, love, and mercy is to be found in our everyday human experience. Laypeople who are called upon to preach can be assured that God is to be found in *their* own, unique life experience. With spouses, families, careers, community responsibilities and a myriad of relationships, laypeople have endless opportunities to experience and name grace in their own lives. They have many ways, over the vast range of human experience—love, joy, pain, suffering, birth, death—to connect life and faith. If they can articulate their experience of God, the community before them will resonate with their experience and be moved to find that "good news" in their own lives. Lay preachers should never feel that they have nothing to share.

In his book *Imaginal Preaching,* James Wallace images the preacher as interpreter[11] and writes that, in that light, the focus of preaching

[10] Mary Catherine Hilkert, *Naming Grace: Preaching and the Sacramental Imagination* (New York: Continuum, 1997) 49.

[11] James A. Wallace, *Imaginal Preaching: An Archetypal Perspective* (New York: Paulist Press, 1995) 14–19.

> is . . . on offering a way to understand the life of the
> community as the arena of God's presence and ongoing
> activity. And the primary instrument employed to arrive
> at such an understanding is the biblical text. The inter-
> preter is the mediator of meaning, the one who moves in
> the "between," standing between scripture texts and the
> people . . .

Lay preachers are most often actively a part of the communities
to whom they minister. They understand the people, their lives,
and the way God works among them because they are part of it
all. On the other hand, the mediation of scriptural meaning can
pose significant challenges for a lay preacher who has not spent
a great deal of time dwelling with the Scriptures. Wallace points
out how important it is for a preacher to meet those challenges.

> [O]ne takes the plunge in order to realize . . . the homily
> is not so much on the Scriptures as from them and through
> them. The homily is not so much an explanation of the
> Scriptures as a process of first entering their world (thus
> speaking from them) and then using this world as a lens
> to look out onto our world (thereby speaking through
> them).

In 1982, the Bishops' Committee on Priestly Life and Ministry of the National Conference of Catholic Bishops published
Fulfilled in Your Hearing: The Homily in the Sunday Assembly.
The booklet is intended to address concerns about the quality
of preaching and to recommended ways to improve preaching
on the national, diocesan and parish levels. Although the intended audience is clergy, lay ministers who are called upon to
reflect publicly on Scripture can benefit enormously from reading it. They might perhaps take heart with its words: "[W]hat
preaching is all about [is] not lofty theological speculation, not
painstaking biblical exegesis, not oratorical flamboyance. The
preacher is a person speaking to people about faith and life."[12]

[12] *Fulfilled in Your Hearing*, 15.

The booklet outlines a method for developing a homily that involves, over the course of a week, reading, listening, praying, studying, drafting, and practicing. A lay preacher might be tempted to think that the method is too involved, too much effort for the little bit of preaching that he or she does. However, the method outlines the care, time and serious work that preaching—regardless of frequency or duration—deserves. It outlines "non-negotiable" elements of effective preaching that are applicable to anyone engaged in this ministry:

Time—The amount will vary depending upon the individual preacher and the sort of preaching, but any preacher—ordained or lay—needs to allocate a significant amount of time to this ministry if it is to be done effectively and well.

Prayer—The prayer life of the preacher is of utmost importance. Prayer is where the connection between life and faith is made.

Study—Ongoing study of Scripture, which can take many forms including individual reading or group reflection, is a professional responsibility for a preacher.

Organization—A homily/reflection needs to have a direction, a focus. A plan and a process of drafting and revising is important.

Concreteness—Rather than vague generalities or lofty theological language, people are nourished by real, concrete, everyday examples of the connections between life and faith. Lay preachers are at no disadvantage here; on the contrary, the very real life experiences of a layperson might in fact lend themselves in a very advantageous way.

Evaluation—Feedback is very important. A lay preacher who has an open, honest, collaborative relationship with the community he or she serves can and should use those lines of communication to solicit and use the input of the community.

Preaching, even when it takes the form of a brief reflection or a dialogue, poses significant challenges for a layperson inexperienced in homiletics. The ministry makes theological, linguistic, and imaginative demands on the preacher. When

approached with care and attention, it can also be richly rewarding.

PART TWO

The Formation of Lay Leaders of Prayer

Overview

Every disciple of the Lord Jesus shares in [his] mission. To do their part, adult Catholics must be mature in faith and well equipped to share the Gospel. . . . They must be women and men of prayer whose faith is alive and vital. . . . Their formation in faith is essential for the Church to carry out its mandate to proclaim the Good News of Jesus to the world. Effective adult formation is necessary to "equip the holy ones for the work of ministry" (Ephesians 4:12).[1]

"Formation in faith" . . . "well equipped to share the Gospel" . . . concepts that apply to all adults, not only ministers. To begin thinking about forming laypeople for ministry, and presiding in particular, it is helpful to begin with a discussion of formation in faith more generally.

There is a tendency among adults in the Church to equate formation in faith with religious education, and in turn to equate that with instruction. For most of us, coming-to-know

---

[1] United States Catholic Bishops, *Our Hearts Were Burning Within Us* (Washington, D.C.: United States Catholic Conference, 1999) 1, 12–13.

in faith has meant reading, studying, and taking in information. Converts to the faith, for example, up until the late twentieth century, were prepared by "taking instruction." While imparting information is an essential part of growing in faith, formation is far more than cognitive. Formation in faith involves experience of God, experience of community, and experience of living a life rooted in the Gospels.

In the earliest Church, those who were preparing for initiation into the Christian faith came to know the faith not only through study but through the experience of being part of a Christian community. Over a period of three years, catechumens were formed in the faith as much by absorbing it from the people around them as by learning it. Spiritual things are more than cognitive. Spiritual things, as St. Paul reminds us, need to be taught "in spiritual terms" (1 Corinthians 2:13)

In the past few decades, the RCIA has returned the modern Church to a more holistic, experiential understanding of initiation and formation in faith. Formation in faith involves the whole person, so any formation program needs to include all that makes us human—our minds, our feelings, our experience. That is done through study, through the witness of others, and through coming to recognize the presence and activity of God in the experience of our own lives.

In 1999, the bishops of this country issued a plan for adult faith formation entitled *Our Hearts Were Burning Within Us.* The plan calls the attention of pastors, parish adult formation leaders, and other parish staff to the need for adult faith formation that will nourish and strengthen lay men and women in their baptismal call as disciples and contributors to the life and work of the Church. The need is pressing, as many adults in the Church today have had little or no religious formation since the sacrament of confirmation when they were children. As a result, many adults in the Church today have an adolescent understanding of their faith and an image of God that is less than mature.

Because our faith is a *living faith*, maturing in faith is an ongoing, lifelong process. A living faith, as the bishops point out, is a *searching faith*, and it "seeks understanding."[2] Adults need to question, probe, critically reflect on, and appropriate for themselves the meaning of God's revelation if they are to come to spiritual maturity. A searching faith leads to an ongoing and ever-deepening journey of conversion. It is reflected in a persistent, trusting, hopeful seeking for a deeper understanding of the Gospel and its power to transform our lives.

Recognizing how multidimensional the task of adult faith formation must be, the bishops outline six dimensions of an effective approach to adult faith formation: (1) knowledge of the faith—Scripture and Church tradition; (2) liturgical life—the sacramental and devotional life of the Church; (3) moral formation—the values of the faith and what they imply for conscience formation; (4) prayer—its various forms, personal and communal; (5) communal life—family, civic, ecclesial, and ecumenical; (6) missionary spirit—the call to evangelize.[3]

The need for adults to grow and mature in their faith is all the more urgent since laypeople are being increasingly relied upon to carry on the work of parish communities, including leading those communities in prayer. This has been the result both of the declining numbers of priests and religious, as well as the changes in the role of laypeople in the Church since Vatican II. Zeni Fox notes that nonordained directors of religious education date back to the mid-1960s. By 1992, a study of people professionally employed in parishes, conducted for the National Conference of Catholic Bishops, found that, in addition to directors of religious education, there were catechists, youth ministers, liturgical ministers, and people acting in other capacities whose job was to carry out the work of the

---

[2] Ibid., 17.
[3] Ibid., 28–33.

parish and pass on the faith.[4] The statistics cited by Fox include people—lay and religious—in professional, paid positions; they do not capture the large increase in laypeople who serve in volunteer capacities as catechists, eucharistic ministers, lectors, and ministers to the sick and homebound. Fox notes that while formation for ministry, with its emphasis on personal and spiritual development, is a valued aspect of seminary life and religious life, opportunities and programs for spiritual formation are not necessarily a component part of degree and certificate programs for laypeople who are preparing for professional ministry in the Church. Lay volunteers in ministry are even less likely to have, or avail themselves of, opportunities for formation for ministry.

The formation of an individual person for ministry begins in their own personal, spiritual life. There can be no substitute for regular habits of prayer, reading, and reflection. An individual's own faith life and relationship with God are the foundation on which ministry is built, and it is essential that they be nurtured. However, formation for ministry should not be left entirely to the individual as a private matter. The communities from which they are called have a role and a stake in their formation. For that reason, dioceses and parishes need to provide opportunities for the formation of lay ministers who are eager to meet the needs of their communities and eager to do that well. That formation needs to go beyond rubrics and skills and take a holistic approach to the needs and growth of ministers.

The model of formation suggested here involves regular meetings that bring lay leaders of prayer together with one another where that is possible, or together with other ministers of the Word, such as lectors and catechists. The model is meant to

[4] Zeni Fox, "Ecclesial Lay Ministers: An Overview," in *Together in God's Service: Toward a Theology of Ecclesial Lay Ministry*, papers from a colloquium by the National Conference of Catholic Bishops, Subcommittee on Lay Ministry, Committee on the Laity (Washington, D.C.: United States Catholic Conference, 1998) 4–5, 10–11.

take the vision in the first part of the book, "Who is the lay leader of prayer?" and offer suggestions about how to begin to make the vision a reality. The model is intended to provide for the formation of leaders of prayer that will give them a sense of the call to ministry that is rooted in their baptism, enhance their understanding of Scripture, strengthen their ministerial identity, and promote their growth toward spiritual maturity. It is meant to stir in the participants an appreciation of their own spiritual depth and an eager ministry of service. It is meant to help them grow not only in ministerial skill but in authenticity, prayerfulness, a spirit of humble service, and openness to the activity of God in their lives.

The model attempts to incorporate some of each of the six dimensions of adult faith formation that the bishops outlined in *Our Hearts Were Burning Within Us*.[5] (1) In writing about the importance of knowledge of the faith as a dimension of adult faith formation, the bishops mention exploring the Scriptures, so that adults might be both "hearers and doers of the Word." While other components of faith knowledge are also important, the model focuses on the scriptural component because the participants are ministers of the Word. (2) The bishops mention the importance of liturgical life in adult faith formation; the model is intended for those who preside at liturgies— Liturgies of the Word with Children, Word and Communion Services, RCIA rites, Liturgy of the Hours, *Sunday Celebration in the Absence of a Priest*. Reflection on their experiences as liturgical ministers is an important component of the formation model. Promoting their awareness of the importance of liturgy and the value of their liturgical ministry is one of the goals of their formation. (3) Moral formation hopefully will be a result of praying with and reflecting on the Scriptures; the bishops specifically mention living a lifestyle reflecting scriptural values as a dimension of adult spiritual formation. This moral formation is the foundation of moral authority and authenticity, as

---

[5] *Our Hearts Were Burning Within Us*, 29–33.

discussed in Part I. (4) The process involves the participants in prayer, both communal prayer to begin and end the sessions and praying with the Scriptures, as an integral component of the meetings. (5) The formation takes place in a group, and hopefully the group process itself promotes a sense of community and provides a source of peer support among the participants. (6) To the extent that the process enhances the ministerial identity of the participants and heightens the sense of their baptismal call to ministry, it will foster a missionary spirit within and among them.

CHAPTER FIVE

Approaches to Adult Spiritual Formation

Having a vision for adult spiritual formation in its many dimensions is not the same as having a plan for how to implement that vision. To develop a plan, it is important to look at what we know about how adults learn. The work that has been done in recent years on adult formation, spiritual formation in particular, has many insights to offer.

Adults learn best when they are in control of the learning process. Rene Bedard's work, "Self-Directed Learning as a New Approach,"[1] describes an approach to adult education which draws upon the experience of the individual, and allows the individual to interpret and be guided by that experience in the process of learning. This is in contrast to a style of learning in which the individual is dependent upon someone in a position of authority to control the learning and dictate what is learned, and in which growth is measured in terms of conformity to norms determined by someone else. Self-directed learning allows the learner to be in control of the learning process, to explore what is happening inside of them while they learn. Both quantitative and qualitative research findings indicate that adult

[1] Rene Bedard, "Self Directed Learning as a New Approach." Marie Gillen and Maurice Taylor, eds., *Adult Religious Education: A Journey of Faith Development* (New York: Paulist Press, 1995) 222–40.

89

learners who are engaged in self-directed learning actually learn more effectively. Bedard also stresses the importance of spiritual experience in spiritual formation, allowing the adult to open up to the self and look inward. This type of self-directed process permits the adult to look within for the resources that ensure that the spiritual journey is real and authentic. Bedard calls spiritual experience the most refined form of religious education and the most significant journey of religious education. It should be stressed that religious experience is a very personal experience; it is a lifelong process that must be respected. Bedard's work would suggest that a program of adult spiritual formation should not be one in which the focus is imparting information from outside sources, but one in which adults are led inward, to listen to Scripture and to put their experiences as ministers into dialogue with our spiritual traditions.

Adults learn best when they share the process with others. Like Bedard, Marge Denis and Brenda Peddigrew emphasize that one of the principles of adult learning is that such learning is an interior process,[2] intuitive and emotional as well as intellectual and rational. Denis and Pedigrew add that effective adult learning is also communal and social. Their work also suggests that adult spiritual formation must respect the inner experience of the learner, and that anything purely lecture-based would not provide an optimal environment for spiritual growth. Denis and Peddigrew's work stresses the importance of community, suggesting that in an ideal environment for spiritual formations, adults will benefit from sharing insights, from drawing on the experiences of others.

Adults learn best in an atmosphere of freedom. It might be stating the obvious to note the importance of comfortable and inviting physical surroundings for adult formation meetings.

---

[2] Marge Denis and Brenda Peddigrew, "Preparing to Facilitate Adult Religious Education." Marie Gillen and Maurice Taylor, eds., *Adult Religious Education: A Journey of Faith Development* (New York: Paulist Press, 1995) 175–201.

What is perhaps not stressed frequently enough, however, is the responsibility of the facilitator to ensure that there is a psychological/emotional environment for the gatherings that is conducive to sharing. When people share from the depths of their being, as they inevitably do in a spiritual conversation, what they share needs to be treated with the utmost respect by everyone present. That respect must be modeled by the facilitator. There must be no hint that anyone's experience is more or less valid than anyone else's, no fear that anyone will be ridiculed or criticized. Differences are potentially enriching if people hold one another in mutual respect. This is fundamentally just Christian respect for one another, but it bears emphasis. People do not learn and grow spiritually in an environment where they feel constrained.

Ideally, adult spiritual formation helps people appreciate the sacredness of all life, to make the connections between—in fact, to integrate—their spiritual lives and their everyday lives. Faith development is not limited to what happens in a weekly or monthly meeting; faith matures as people live their lives intentionally grounded in their faith. This suggests that a successful approach to adult spiritual formation will give the participants tools for that integration, methods of making those connections.

Research on approaches to adult formation provide some helpful guidelines for how to develop a process that will contribute to the spiritual and ministerial growth of lay leaders of prayer. Within those broad guidelines, there is abundant room for choosing particular methods and formats. An individual program can be tailored to the needs of the participants and the resources of the community. The model suggested below takes the guidelines as a framework and gives it shape and texture.

CHAPTER SIX

A Model Formation Program

Having explored a vision of the spirituality of the lay presider and the components of ministerial identity, it remains to bring those ideas together with what we know about adult spiritual formation and to put flesh and bones on a formation program. What follows is the outline of what a formation program for lay leaders of prayer might look like in practice. It assumes that the individual minister will also continue to build a foundation of regular prayer, reading and reflection. This model could be implemented on the parish or diocesan level. Alternatively, in the absence of diocesan or parish involvement, lay leaders of prayer could implement such a program themselves by coming together as a group, perhaps with other ministers of the Word. The model suggested here is of course not exhaustive, but is meant to be suggestive. A formation program should, in practice, be tailored and adapted to the needs of the ministers it serves.[1]

[1] The comments in this chapter are those of ministers of the Word who participated in a six-month formation program in my home parish. The program was a pilot study on which my doctoral dissertation was based. The ministers included lay presiders, lectors, and catechists.

Regular Meetings

Regular meetings among those who preside at prayer can be extremely beneficial. In a parish setting, leaders of prayer of all kinds can gather together and those meetings can bear fruit for each of their ministries. Those who preside at Children's Liturgies of the Word, for example, can benefit from the perspectives of those who preside at Word and Communion Services, Liturgy of the Hours, or other services for adults. If the numbers are too few, leaders of prayer might come together with clergy or other ministers of the Word such as lectors or catechists. The latter ministries have much in common with leading prayer, and ministers could benefit from the different perspectives that would be brought to such a mixed group. As one parish minister who participated in such a program said:

> Ideally, all Ministers of the Word would be involved in a program like this. Deeper involvement of the laity in the work of the Church is a wonderful characteristic of our contemporary Church, yet we don't have a sense that preparation and ongoing education is required. [This program] is a major step forward.

Another said: "What I liked the best was the opportunity to experience the spirituality of other members of the parish in a more immediate way." And another added, "More heads, more involvement, means more input!"

At a diocesan level, leaders of *Sunday Celebrations in the Absence of a Priest* might be brought together for more than just organizational meetings. One meeting a month devoted to formation would provide a resource that is difficult to find elsewhere and difficult to do without.

The meetings, if they are an hour and a half to two hours long, might be divided into two parts: reflection on Scripture and reflection on ministry. Structure in a meeting, if it is not rigid, lends a degree of predictability and helps people to feel comfortable since, to at least some extent, they know what to expect and what will be asked of them.

Meetings should begin and end with prayer, and if the participants take turns being responsible for the prayer it is yet another opportunity to practice the ministry of presiding and a chance to become a little more comfortable giving voice to the prayer of a group.

Reflection on Scripture can be done in a variety of ways, but since the ministers involved are likely to be doing something Lectionary-based, focus on the Sunday Scriptures can be helpful in practical as well as spiritual ways. If leaders of prayer and/or other ministers of the Word reflect on the Scriptures that will be directly involved in their ministries—preaching, teaching, or proclamation—the work of their ministry, in addition to their spiritual lives, can only be enriched by the experience.

If the *lectio divina* approach is used, the readings for a month of Sundays can, if the meeting moves along at a steady pace, be covered in an hour and a half. This would suggest meetings at monthly intervals. A more leisurely pace would suggest a more ambitious schedule of weekly or biweekly meetings. The meetings should provide a structure for reflection on the Scriptures that allows the reflection to be directed by the participants. Anything lecture-based on this regular basis, while no doubt imparting valuable information, would not be self-directed and would not draw on the actual, lived experience of the participants. One parish minister who took part in a program like this said: "I came really wanting to increase my knowledge of the Scriptures, and that has happened." Another said: "*Lectio divina* calls my attention to particular words and phrases in Scripture that I would otherwise probably miss. It's especially helpful that we read the passages twice, since sometimes it takes a second reading to understand them." Another said: "This program has developed my spiritual involvement and participation. It encouraged me to put more time into understanding the Scriptures—which I have overlooked before.

I have a hard time with feeling that I have identity as a minister, and these meetings help to remind me who I am."

A break for refreshments seems like a trivial thing to mention, but the time spent sharing food is time for the participants to get to know one another on a more personal level, time for forming relationships. This adds to the formation program as a source of support, and the sharing involved in the rest of the meetings can only benefit if the participants become more comfortable with one another. Spiritual sharing among friends flows much more freely and easily than it does among strangers.

The second part of the meeting could focus on the experience of ministry, with an effort to make the reflection theological rather than just practical. The structure need not be rigid, but some structure is important, since reflection on ministry can take off in many different directions. The facilitator must take care to keep the discussion on a fruitful track. The participants might take turns, one each meeting, in relating an experience in their ministry and reflecting on it with the group. For example, a leader of prayer might bring to the group for reflection an incident in his or her ministry that called for flexibility and improvisation. Or one might bring to the group for discussion an incident where his or her ministry was challenged or openly objected to and how he or she responded. The input and support of the group can provide a mirror, a sounding board, and an opportunity for growth as a minister. It is important for the facilitator to move the discussion to a theological level as well as a pastoral level, so that ministry and our faith tradition can be connected in the lives and work of the participants. Two different approaches to theological reflection were mentioned in chapter 4. The particular method for making the reflection theological is less important than the effort to do so. Theological reflection helps the participants to see their work not just as tasks but as ministry.

An alternative approach would be for each participant to take a turn, one at each meeting, to bring a videotape of themselves leading prayer, for the group to critique. It is helpful if the discussion is structured. This can be done by the subject of the videotape asking the group for input on specific aspects of what they did, or posing specific questions to the group. Again, the group can be a valuable mirror and sounding board, offering encouragement and pointing out things that the individual minister might not have thought of alone. It would be important for the facilitator to insist that any input be constructive and supportive. Even criticism and correction can be offered in positive ways.

A third possible approach would be to choose a topic for the meeting and invite some reflection by all of the participants. For example, ministers could be invited one week to talk about their sense of authority for ministry; another week about how ministry has transformed them. Over time, topics are likely to emerge from the discussions themselves. Gender issues might be on the minds of participants, or something more specific like the faith life of children. The needs of the group can and should give rise to the topics selected. Again, an effort should be made to give the reflection and discussion a theological dimension, to place the topics in the context not only of pastoral work but of our faith tradition. One parish minister commented on this approach: "The first activity [Scripture reflection] is something I do weekly in a prayer group. The second [reflection on ministry] is more appealing because I've never really addressed these issues alone or in a group." Another said: "I have extensive experience as a leader of prayer (parish, chaplaincy, intentional eucharistic community) but look forward to these sessions for deepening formation." Another said: "I love having this spiritual nourishment for myself. It naturally spills over into my ministry."

Sample Schedule for an Evening Formation Meeting

7:00–7:10   Opening Prayer

7:10–8:15   Reflection on Sunday Scriptures

8:15–8:30   Break, refreshments, time for friendship

8:30–8:45   Presentation of an incident in ministry or videotape

8:45–9:15   Group discussion of an incident/tape/topic

9:15–9:30   Agreement on topics, etc. for next meeting; closing prayer

Workshops

As part of a formation program, workshops can be offered to supplement the spiritual growth that is the purpose of the small-group sharing. Workshops can provide an explicitly instructional component to a formation program. They can also provide the opportunity to explore subject areas that Scripture reflection and theological reflection on ministry might not touch upon. Workshops should not, in general, replace the regular meetings. They can be held at a time separate from the regular meeting.

Workshops can be more lecture-based, although it is critical to allow time for information to be questioned, challenged, processed, and integrated with individual experience. Topics can be chosen to meet the particular needs of the group. Any group of ministers of the Word, for example, would benefit from a workshop on the interpretation of Scripture, or public speaking and the use of the voice. Presiders who work with the elderly would benefit from hearing from an expert in the spiritual life of the elderly, and similarly with ministers who preside at liturgies with children. A workshop on liturgy, its forms and its symbols, is helpful for any liturgical ministers. The topics are as many and as varied as the needs of the group. If a parish or diocese hires speakers to provide the workshops, they might be opened to attendance by others so as to maximize their benefits.

While the sharing that takes place at the regular meetings can work best with a more clearly defined group of people who have come to know one another and bonded, the lectures could be open to attendance by others in the parish or diocese. The topics of the workshops might be of more general interest and benefit people in other ministries.

Evaluative Tools

Those responsible for the formation of leaders of prayer might understandably want a way to measure progress, to tell whether their efforts are having an effect. To begin to approach an evaluation of the effectiveness of a formation program such as this, it is helpful to turn to research in pastoral care and counseling. Providing an opportunity for formation can be characterized as an "intervention" in the spiritual and ministerial life a person, and evaluated in much the same way that social scientists might evaluate the effects of intervention such as pastoral counseling or psychotherapy.

The evaluation formation program must be responsive to the spoken and unspoken expectations of the people it addresses and include the opportunity for participants to evaluate themselves. Experts in the field of pastoral care and counseling have cited some religious/ theological variables that can help to pinpoint individual needs and expectations and to do justice to the uniqueness of the individuals being evaluated. For example, assessments can attempt to evaluate a person's (1) awareness of the holy. Where is God at work in their life? What is their sense of God's presence and providence? (2) A person's sense of vocation can be explored, their sense of their active participation in the world and the scheme of creation, their sense of living with a purpose. What is God's intention for them? What is God calling them to do? (3) A person's sense of community can also be addressed, their sense of belonging and their sense of their role in the community. These are admittedly difficult issues to explore with specificity. They cannot be objectively verified but can only be assessed by relying on sensitive questions and careful listening as a person reveals their sense of who they are at the deepest core of their being. Questionnaires and other

mechanical diagnoses are of only limited value. They can, however, provide those with responsibility for the formation of
ministers some valuable insights.

The questionnaire suggested here is an attempt to assess a
person's feelings about their role in the community, their sense
of call/vocation, their confidence in doing the work of ministry,
and their identity as ministers. The assessment tool suggested
here focuses on three variables and three sources of data. The
particular variables are (1) the confidence with which a minister
approaches his or her particular ministry, which for a minister
of the Word includes their confidence in their grasp of Scripture and their confidence in discussing and publicly reflecting
on Scripture; (2) the minister's awareness of a connection between their ministry and their own spiritual life, which is really
about their sense of call and vocation and their authenticity as
ministers; (3) the individual's identity as a minister, which en-
compasses how readily they perceive themselves as being seen
as a leader of prayer for the community, a servant of the community, and a reflection of the image of God for the community. The sources of data are these questionnaires, which the
participants can be asked to fill out before the process begins
(to establish a baseline) and then at periodic intervals throughout the formation program.

The questionnaires are an attempt to measure the effectiveness of the program in enhancing the confidence of the participants as leaders of prayer, in fostering the connection between
their ministry and their own spiritual life, and in developing
their identity as ministers. The first part of the questionnaires
asked for numerical responses on a scale of 0 to 5, in an attempt
to make response quick and easy, and also to provide some con-
sistent means of measurement over time. The questionnaires
also pose open-ended questions to which the participants can
write comments and detailed responses if they choose. Anonymity is not essential, but the option of not signing their
name might leave the participants feeling freer to be honest
and open in their answers.

Sample Questionnaire

Please let your answer to each question take the form of a number:

0 = never
1 = rarely or almost none of the time
2 = a little of the time
3 = some of the time
4 = a good part of the time
5 = most or all of the time
6 = this item does not apply

I feel confident as a leader of prayer _____

I feel confident of my ability to understand Scripture _____

I feel confident when I preach/give a reflection on Scripture _____

I feel a connection between my ministry as a leader of prayer and my own prayer/spiritual life _____

When I preside at prayer, I feel as though I am

The focal point of hospitality for those gathered _____

The focal point of unity for those gathered _____

One who prays in the name of the community _____

A servant of the community _____

One who images Christ for the community _____

Please let your answer to the following questions take the form of a number:

    1—agree
    2—agree somewhat
    3—disagree somewhat
    4—strongly disagree
    5—does not apply

As a result of my participation in the program:

My confidence as a minister has increased   _____

My knowledge of Scripture has increased   _____

My ability to reflect on Scripture has increased   _____

My sense of identity as a minister has increased   _____

My own spiritual life has deepened   _____

I would recommend that the program be continued   _____

My favorite part of being a presider is

My least favorite part of being a presider is

Other comments that you would like to share:

While the open-ended questions provide some valuable insights, the numerical responses are useful because they can be compiled to form a time series of data for each participant as well as a cross-section of data across participants. Movements in the numbers, even more than the numbers themselves, can be indicative of the effects the formation program is having.

The first three questions on the questionnaires are intended to discern the minister's confidence as a minister of the Word. The first question is a simple, direct question about the confidence they feel in their role. The second two questions are intended to discern their confidence/comfort level with Scripture: understanding of Scripture and sharing reflections on Scripture. The third question asks about confidence in preaching, the particular way in which presiders are called to share their thoughts on Scripture.

The fourth question asks how strong a connection the minister felt between his or her ministry and personal, spiritual life. It is aimed at discerning their feeling of authenticity as a minister. It is also an attempt to discern, over time, whether the presider's awareness of the importance of their own spiritual life in their ministry is growing.

The final set of five questions is an attempt to discern the minister's sense of identity as a minister. These questions are more specific than the first question that asked about overall confidence. Presiders are asked whether they feel that they are the focal point of hospitality and the focal point of unity for the community when they lead at prayer. The presiders are asked if they feel that they pray in the name of the community, whether they feel like a servant of the community, and whether they feel as though they image Christ for the community.

The questionnaires and the responses they generate are not ends in themselves, but tools for assessing how the formation program is working. Considered as time series, the data might be used by a parish or diocese for periodic evaluation and revision of the program as an approach to formation. Over time, it is hoped that the participants would show some increase in ministerial identity, confidence in the work of ministry, and sense of connection between ministry and their spiritual life. If not, discussion with the participants about the strengths and weaknesses of the program, in light of their particular needs, would be warranted.

Individual participants might also benefit from seeing how their responses to questions change over time. The questions themselves give the participants focus for reflection. They can offer the participants some insights into their strengths, weaknesses, and needs for growth as ministers.

A Renewed Vision of Spiritual Leadership

Prayer is where we, as Christians, go to draw life. When our spirits are parched, we go to prayer to drink deeply of the living water of God's love. Prayer is where God feeds our hunger and quenches our thirst. The one who leads a community in prayer is one who has drawn life from that Source, hungered and thirsted for God and been satisfied. The one who leads a community in prayer is one with a deep and rich spiritual life of their own and one who allows it to be life-giving for others. The one who leads a community in prayer needs to be nourished and supported by the community he or she serves, to develop and hone the skills necessary for effective leadership.

Why should laypeople who are called upon to lead prayer pay careful attention to their own their spiritual life? Why should the community be concerned about their identity as ministers? Why do we, as a Church, have a stake in the formation of leaders of prayer? There are many reasons. Let me offer a few.

Ministry is more than a function; it involves the whole person. A minister can only give what he or she has. To be a witness to God's presence and an image of that presence for the community, a leader of prayer must have experienced that presence at the very core of their being. To proclaim God's love with conviction, a minister must have felt that love in the depths of their soul. To call a community to transformation by the Word of God, the leader of prayer must have taken that Word to heart and allowed it to take root there. It is a minister's own spiritual life that grounds the work of their ministry, and as an icon and a prophetic witness, a minister needs to be firmly grounded.

The ministry of presiding is demanding and difficult, and it changes the minister. It shapes the minister's answers to the questions, "Who is God?" and "Who am I?" As with any other role in life, as with any other life-shaping choices that we make, sometimes lay presiders will find themselves wondering why they ever chose to do this. It might be a passing thought, or it might continue for a considerable length of time. When call and vocation feel tentative and shaky, when the demands seem overwhelming, leaders of prayer must be firmly grounded in their identity as ministers in order to deal with what is happening.

Lay leaders of prayer sometimes find their ministry questioned, objected to, and even openly opposed. Their very right to do it is sometimes challenged. When that occurs, leaders of prayer need to be firmly grounded in their identity as ministers to deal gracefully, respectfully, and steadfastly with what is happening.

Not only do individual ministers have a stake in ministerial identity. The Church as a community has a responsibility to form its ministers. Far from a grudging acceptance of lay leadership of prayer as a necessity, the Church has an opportunity to embrace it as a gift to the Church and as prophetic witness. The landscape of ministry is changing. There are fewer priests and religious to meet the growing needs of our growing communities. As a Church, we have in this moment the opportunity to affirm that spiritual leaders are called forth from the community, and that gifts of spiritual leadership are not limited to the ordained. As a Church, we also have the opportunity in this moment to reaffirm the dignity and the gifts of all the baptized, and in a particular way the dignity of women, since so many lay leaders of prayer are women.

The growing reliance on lay people for leadership of prayer is an opportunity for the Church as a community of faith, an opportunity to open new dimensions of our vision of spiritual leadership. As Jesus promised, the seeds of the kingdom are among us.

Bibliography

Aschenbrenner, George. "A Hidden Self Grown Strong." In Robert J. Wicks, ed. *Handbook of Spirituality for Ministers.* New York: Paulist Press, 1995.

Beal, John, James Coriden, and Thomas Green. *New Commentary on the Code of Canon Law.* New York: Paulist Press, 2000.

Bedard, Rene. "Self-Directed Learning as a New Approach." In Marie Gillen and Maurice Taylor, eds. *Adult Religious Education: A Journey of Faith Development.* New York: Paulist Press, 1995.

Begolly, Michael. *Leading the Assembly in Prayer: A Practical Guide for Lay and Ordained Presiders.* San Jose, California: Resource Publications, 1997.

Bergant, Dianne. "Biblical Foundations for Christian Ministry." In *Together in God's Service: Toward a Theology of Ecclesial Lay Ministry.* Washington, D.C.: National Conference of Catholic Bishops, 1998.

Bernier, Paul. *Ministry in the Church: A Historical and Pastoral Approach.* Mystic, Connecticut: Twenty-Third Publications, 1996.

Brillinger, Margaret Fisher. "Adult Learning in a Religious Context." In Marie Gillen and Maurice Taylor, eds. *Adult Religious Education: A Journey of Faith Development.* New York: Paulist Press, 1995.

Denis, Marge, and Brenda Peddigrew. "Preparing to Facilitate Adult Religious Education." In Marie Gillen and Maurice Taylor, eds. *Adult Religious Education: A Journey of Faith Development.* New York: Paulist Press, 1995.

Dreyer, Elizabeth. *Earth Crammed with Heaven: A Spirituality of Everyday Life.* New York: Paulist Press, 1994.

Fink, Peter. "Spirituality for Liturgical Presiders." In Eleanor J. Bernstien, ed. *Disciples at the Crossroads: Perspectives on Worship and Church Leadership.* Collegeville, Minnesota: The Liturgical Press, 1993.

Fitchett, George. *Spiritual Assessment in Pastoral Care: A Guide to Selected Resources.* JPCP Monograph No. 4. Decatur, Georgia: Journal of Pastoral Care Publications, 1993.

Fox, Zeni. "Ecclesial Lay Ministers: An Overview." In *Together in God's Service: Toward a Theology of Ecclesial Lay Ministry.* National Conference of Catholic Bishops, Subcommittee on Lay Ministry, Washington, D.C.: National Conference of Catholic Bishops, 1998.

Gillen, Marie A., and Maurice C. Taylor. *Adult Religious Education: A Journey of Faith Development.* New York: Paulist Press, 1995.

Hilkert, Mary Catherine. *Naming Grace: Preaching and the Sacramental Imagination.* New York: Continuum, 1998.

Hovda, Robert W. *Strong, Loving, and Wise: Presiding in Liturgy.* Collegeville, Minnesota: The Liturgical Press, 1976.

Huck, Gabe. *Liturgy with Style and Grace.* Chicago: Liturgy Training Publications, 1987.

Hughes, Kathleen. *Lay Presiding: The Art of Leading Prayer.* Collegeville, Minnesota: The Liturgical Press, 1991.

International Commission on English in the Liturgy. *Book of Blessings.* Collegeville, Minnesota: The Liturgical Press, 1989.

Kinast, Robert. *Making Faith Sense: Theological Reflection in Everyday Life.* Collegeville, Minnesota: The Liturgical Press, 1999.

Morris, Thomas. "The Ministry of the Baptized: Reclaiming the Call." *Assembly* 16 (1) (October 1989) 460–64.

National Conference of Catholic Bishops. *Our Hearts Were Burning Within Us.* Washington, D.C.: United States Catholic Conference, 1999.

National Conference of Catholic Bishops, Committee on the Liturgy. *Sunday Celebrations in the Absence of a Priest.* New York: Catholic Book Publishing Company, 1994.

National Conference of Catholic Bishops, Committee on Priestly Life and Ministry. *Fulfilled in Your Hearing: The Homily in the Sunday Assembly.* Washington, D.C.: United States Catholic Conference, 1982.

Nouwen, Henry. *Bread for the Journey: A Daybook of Wisdom and Faith.* San Francisco: Harper, 1997.

Power, David. *The Eucharistic Mystery.* New York: Crossroad, 1995.

Rosser, Aelred. *Guide for Lectors.* Chicago: Liturgy Training Publications, 1998.

VaneCreek, Larry, Hilary Bender, and Merle Jordan. *Research in Pastoral Care and Counseling: Quantitative and Qualitative Approaches.* Decatur, Georgia: Journal of Pastoral Care Publications, 1994.

Vatican Council II. Dogmatic Constitution on the Church. (November 1964).

Vatican Offices. "Some Questions Regarding Collaboration of Non-ordained Lay Faithful in Priests' Sacred Ministries." (November 1997).

Vest, Norvene. *Gathered in the Word: Praying the Scriptures in Small Groups.* Nashville, Tennessee: Upper Room Books, 1996.

Walsh, Eugene. "Training the Muscles That Celebrate." *Liturgy* 17 (6) (1972).

Whitehead, James D., and Evelyn Eaton Whitehead. *Method in Ministry: Theological Reflection and Christian Ministry.* Kansas City, Missouri: Sheed and Ward, 1995.